How to Succeed in College

How to
Succeed
in College

Marcia K. Johnson
Sally P. Springer
Sarah Hall Sternglanz

William Kaufmann, Inc.
Los Altos, California

Library of Congress Cataloging in Publication Data

Johnson, Marcia K.
  How to succeed in college.

  Bibliography: p.
  Includes index.
  1. College students—Conduct of life.
2. Study, Method of. I. Springer, Sally P.,
1947-   . II. Sternglanz, Sarah Hall, 1942-
III. Title.
LB3605.J54   378'.198   82-15240
ISBN 0-86576-035-7   AACR2

10 9 8 7 6 5 4 3 2 1

Printed in the United States of America

Contents

To our students

1.

Why You Should Read This Book

Who Is This Book For?

This book is for people who want the inside scoop about how college works, for people who don't want to go through college the hard way.

Whoever you are, this book is for you if you are a student who hates
- Panic
- Confusion
- Depression
- Loneliness
- Feeling pushed around

It's for you if you want to
- Get the most out of your classes
- Do well on exams
- Get to know your professors
- Make friends and have time for fun
- Get a good job or go on to grad school

As you can see, this book is meant for just about every college student. It suggests answers for problems like those listed above and others (such as getting through the maze of college requirements and taking lecture notes) that are shared by almost *all* students. Now, you also might be special in some way—returning after years of working or raising a family, handicapped, trying to overcome a poor high school education, or commuting to and from campus. This book can help you if you have one or more of these special problems.

Whether you are a high school student about to enter college for the first time or starting your junior year, whether you are in a four-year university or a two-year college, whether your college is large or small, this book can help you get off to a good start, get back on the right track, or simply make a good thing even better.

What Makes Us Think We Can Help You?

We've helped lots of other students. We are three professors. Together, our experience includes almost 30 years of teaching—everything from large lecture courses with 600 students down to small seminars with only 10. We figure we have had contact of one sort or another with at least 3000 undergraduates. In our years of teaching, we've spent many hours talking to students about the sorts of problems and pressures they face and how they deal with them. All professors do some of this, but we've spent even more time than most because each of us has been in charge of an advising program at a large university.

In addition, we were all undergraduates once ourselves. We went to college on the East Coast and on the West Coast. Our living arrangements included living at home with parents, as well as in dorms, a sorority house, a boarding house, and an apartment. Among us, we went to a community college (both day and evening classes), an Ivy League private school, and state universities. One of us had a nearly straight-A average, and one of us had a somewhat more "colorful" record. We were financed by parents. We worked. Two of us went straight through in four years. One of us "stopped out." Obviously, we were all students who eventually mastered the "system."

For a long time we have felt it would be helpful to put in writing the information we've collected and have been sharing with our students. Some of the information is straightforward fact, and some is a little more subtle. For example, many students don't know how to approach a professor about a change of grade. They feel they deserve more credit on an exam, but they don't know how to handle the situation and so deal with it awkwardly or not at all. (See Chapter 7 to find out how to do it right.)

Some problems, though, don't have such simple solutions, for example, how to balance personal and academic pressures. One-to-one counseling for any problem can be useful, if only because it helps to tell someone about your troubles and to feel someone cares about you in particular. However, many students do not seek out this kind of contact with faculty, and many colleges and/or professors are not able to provide it. And even if you do have a chance to talk to a professor or counselor, that person may not have the time to explain some things in detail (such as how to study more effectively) or may never have given much thought to certain other problems (such as what to do if a professor makes a pass at you).

We felt that if we combined our experience in a book, we could offer some ideas about how to approach the kinds of problems you run into at college.

Take a few minutes to look over the Table of Contents and read through the first paragraph of each chapter. This is the best way to find out what we have included, so you can decide what you want to read (and in what order).

Most of the book will apply to almost everyone, but there are special sections you will either want to read or leave out, depending on your needs.

For example, new students who are about to enter college may want to start with Chapter 9, "Away or at Home—Where Should You Live?," because it gives some useful tips about things to think about in advance. Continuing students who are thinking about a change in their living arrangements might also want to read this chapter, because of the way it compares different housing options. Finally, commuting students will benefit from the sections dealing with the special advantages and disadvantages of living at home while going to college.

If you're not sure what to read, start at the beginning and read right through. That's the best way to make sure you don't miss anything.

Is There a Basic Message Here?

Yes. You can have more control over what happens to you at college than you may think. Read on.

2.

Getting Started

The few days just before classes start and the few days right after are probably the busiest and most important of the school year. It's a time to get settled in and to make decisions about your program that will affect you the entire term.

If you are a freshman, everything will be new to you. If you are a transfer student, you've had some experience, but there are still many things that will be different and unfamiliar at your new college. This chapter will help you get off to a good start. In fact, it contains a lot of information and hints that can be of help even to a student who has been around for awhile and plans to stay at the same college.

Survey the Terrain

Spend some time walking around the campus to get a feel for the place. The catalog will usually have a map of the campus—use it to find out where the important places are. Go by the cafeteria and the student union and note the hours. Find out where there is a check-cashing service and when it is open. Another place you should visit in advance of classes, if possible, is the bookstore; it can be a great help to you in choosing your courses (see pages 14-15 later in this chapter).

Locate the buildings where the courses you want to take are being given and develop a plan for your first day of classes. If you know in advance how to get from one place to the next, you will be there on time. If you arrive on time and there's a first come, first served basis for allowing students into class, you'll be more likely to get in.

Part of your tour of the campus should include looking for notices about orientation meetings. Special sessions are usually advertised for freshmen or transfer students where a faculty member, administrator, or advanced student explains requirements and gives out useful information. Go to these. It's worth the time and effort, and it's an efficient way to find out what's going on. Also look for notices of parties and "mixers" for freshmen, commuters, or other groups; they are a good way to meet people.

Visit the Library

Go to the library and find out if tours on "how to use the library" are given. Your campus may even have more than one library. On some campuses, there are separate libraries for many of the different departments, such as math, physics, psychology, and so forth, in addition to the main library. Most students do not know how to use the library when they arrive at the college, because a college library is much more complex than the one they remember from their neighborhood or high school. Take advantage of a tour if one is available.

Read Everything

Get into the habit of reading the notices on any door before entering. Directions to important offices are often posted in this way, especially during the first week of classes.

A lot of information on college campuses is exchanged by notices posted on bulletin boards — where to find apartments, how to get typing services, cars for sale, rides to the nearest city, as well as where classes are meeting, changes in departmental requirements, etc. Browse through the signs on bulletin boards and read the notices posted outside of departmental offices and on faculty doors regularly. The campus newspaper is also a good source of announcements as well as advertisements about where to buy a cheap hamburger.

The *least* efficient way to get the information you'll need during the first week is to wander into the nearest faculty office and ask. Chances are you will be disturbing someone, and you won't get an accurate answer anyway. There is no reason, for example, why Professor Jones should know where you can find Professor Smith if Professor Smith isn't in her office.

Planning Your Program

You've settled into your dorm, met your roommate(s), and taken yourself on an informal campus tour. The place seems friendly enough, and you are looking forward to classes starting. You have one problem, though. You don't have a good answer to the question you're being asked with alarming frequency—What courses are you taking?

Actually, you are not alone. Over half of the freshman class would probably answer, "I don't know. I don't understand the catalog or the requirements. I don't know what I'm majoring in, and I can't read the computerized course schedule. I have five pounds of preregistration material, and I don't know what to do with any of it." Because so much else is going on, you might be tempted to sign up for whatever your friends or roommates are taking and to put off any planning until some other, less busy time. This is a mistake. It is really worth spending an hour or two planning your first year and looking as far into the future as you can.

In this section we will discuss some of the things you should consider in your planning, as well as define some terms everyone assumes you know but that may sound like Greek to you. It will help you concentrate on what is important in working out a program and how to go about doing it. We don't advise, though, that you plan your program your first term (or any term, for that matter) entirely by yourself. All colleges realize that new students need some help, and they provide it in the form of freshman or orientation counseling.

Your college may have a program of large orientation meetings, or perhaps they set up appointments for students to meet with counselors individually. Some do both. Take advantage of these. There will be an opportunity to ask questions. Our hints are good ones that should apply anywhere, but we can't give you all the detailed information you'll need since colleges differ.

Distribution Requirements

Many colleges have a list of required courses that must be taken by everyone who expects to get a degree. These are sometimes called "college wide" or **distribution** requirements and are usually listed in the college catalog. Although these requirements are less rigid than they were in the past, most colleges still list certain courses or categories of courses that you must take.

The idea behind these college-wide requirements is that there is certain knowledge that all educated members of a society should share, regardless of what they do for a living. This knowledge, which includes a background in (among other things) history, philosophy, literature, and basic scientific principles, is often referred to as a "liberal education."

One or two of your courses each semester should help you fulfill these college-wide requirements. If a math course is among the possibilities, consider taking this your first year. A basic college math course is often required before you can take many other courses. If you are afraid of math, your college may have special courses for you.

Requirements for Your Major

In addition to fulfilling distribution requirements, most colleges require you to choose a major. A **major** is a field you have decided to study in depth, such as biology, physics, or French, and each major requires specific courses. Some colleges let you plan a major that cuts across the traditional lines that divide knowledge into "departments." For example, you might be able to major in "social science." The major, of course, is not the only thing a student studies at college, but it is his or her area of concentration. Some colleges also require the student to have a **minor**. The minor is an area of concentration in which the student takes fewer courses than they do in their major but where there is still a substantial amount of course work. It is a good idea to become familiar with the kinds of courses required by different majors. Few students are ready to choose a major during their first year, but it is not too soon to start thinking about possibilities. Chapter 13 will go into choosing a major in more detail.

In your first term you might want to take an introductory course in a field that might become your major. Most majors have an introductory freshman-level course (or courses—sometimes it is a two-term sequence). In some departments there is also a freshman course for non-majors. Don't take a non-majors course unless you are *sure* you won't want to major in the field or take further courses in it. A course for non-majors is usually not a satisfactory foundation (or "prerequisite") for advanced courses in that field. Pay careful attention to the prerequisites listed for all the courses you are thinking of taking. **Prerequisites** are courses you must have taken in the past before you can register for a course. The list of requirements gives you important information about the kind of background the courses will require. Most introductory courses, however, do not have any prerequisites—they can be taken by anyone.

When you take an introductory-level course in a field that may become your major, keep two things in mind. One is that you should put the most work into this course since your grades in your major will be important later. The other is that this is a chance to take a serious look at an area to see whether you might enjoy it for four or more years. Students often do not know what kind of course work a major involves. People majoring in psychology study statistics and rat learning as well as abnormal human behavior. Music majors often spend more time in composition and appreciation classes than they do playing instruments. Premedical students take organic chemistry and physics; they rarely have anything to do with hospitals as part of their official program.

Class Size

You probably won't have much choice when it comes to class size. Freshman courses are usually the largest on campus and the most likely to be taught with multiple-choice tests and little contact with the professor. Fortunately, small classes aren't essential for good teaching in all subjects. Often, large classes are taught by people with a flair for teaching large groups, so the instructor's ability may make up for the lack of personal contact. If personal attention is important to you in a large class, sign up for one that breaks up into discussion or lab sections on a regular basis. Your section leader can frequently provide you with the personal attention that is lacking in a large course.

Professors' Reputations

Most schools have some type of student course evaluation form to be filled out at the end of each term. In some schools the results are published, and you can read what last year's students thought of specific courses and professors. If evaluations are not available, you will have to ask around. Unless you find several people agreeing that a professor is superb or horrible, don't let casual comments influence you too much. If, however, a course you want to take is being taught by someone everyone agrees is terrible, consider waiting a year (if it's not the introductory course in your major or otherwise essential). Sometimes professors take turns teaching courses, and you may be able to take the course from someone else.

Your Other Interests

Take some courses that are of interest to you even if they are not "useful." Not everything has to relate in an obvious way to your major, a future job, or graduate school. You have four years in which your "job" is to become as well-rounded and broadly educated as possible. If you know nothing about art, consider taking an art appreciation course. If political science is a mystery to you, think about an introductory course. If you've always been interested in dinosaurs and cavemen, take physical anthropology or archaeology.

Unless you are very lucky, very wealthy, or very organized, your college years will probably be the last time in your life that you will have this much time and energy to spend on developing yourself as a person. Don't stick to your narrow professional field or what you did well in during high school — take a chance on something new. If you are worried about your grades, think about taking some courses on a **Pass-Fail** (or **Pass-No Credit**) basis rather than for a letter grade. Many colleges let you do this to encourage you to explore new areas. A schedule with too many courses from the same area is like a meal where the food is all alike — you get full fast! Taking courses in a variety of areas each term may be good for your grades by helping to stimulate you and keep your interest up.

Keeping Doors Open

This is probably the most important point of all. If you don't know what you want to major in, take basic courses that leave you as many options as possible (and take them for letter grades, not Pass-Fail). Even if you do know your major, you may change your mind. Leave yourself that option. If you don't take calculus your first year, for instance, you may eliminate many majors unless you are willing to take calculus later. This may keep you in college longer. Are you so sure that your intended major is what you want or that the way it is taught at your school makes it your best choice? Give some thought to what your second choice might be and leave it open.

How Much Work Are These Courses?

Try not to overload yourself at any point, but especially not in your first year. Some common overloads are:

Too Many Labs

A laboratory course takes more time than many other courses. It is constant work, preparing, running, and writing up the experiments. You usually have a lab report due every week; these may be ten pages each and may have to be written in a particular style. Learning this style can take several weeks, during which time you may have to rewrite your old lab reports. One lab course per term is all most people should take.

Too Many Courses Directly Related to Your Major

Yet another good reason to take courses unrelated to your major (aside from broadening your education) is that if you need to put less effort into one course, it's nice to be registered for some subject in which a lower grade won't hurt you. Of course, you may start by aiming for A's all around, but if you break an arm or your heart halfway through the term, you will be glad that it's clear which course has the lowest priority.

Unbalanced Workload

Different courses offered by different instructors have different amounts and types of work. Choose courses that look fairly easy in terms of formal requirements to mix with those that require three papers and three exams. Check the **syllabus** or course outline. If the papers for two different courses are due the same day, obviously you won't be able to wait until the last week to write them both.

Seek Out Challenging Courses

You may not have the nerve for this your first term, but if all has gone well then you should certainly try to find courses that challenge you. It is particularly important to find courses that let you write a lot. Writing is one of the most important skills you will learn or practice in college; it is useful in any career. Don't wind up with a tremendous skill in taking multiple-choice tests and nothing else (they don't use many multiple-choice tests in the "real" world—but they do ask you to write). The writing you do does not have to be in creative writing courses. Your goal should be clarity, and you can learn that from writing lab reports, term papers, or take-home essay exams.

There are other kinds of challenges, of course, besides writing well. Take some courses in fields that scare you a little—math or sight-reading music or French conversation or new-criticism English courses. Learn karate or how to swim. Take the courses Pass-Fail if you can and want to so that you don't have the excuse of worrying about your grade. Try new things—you'll be surprised at yourself.

Scheduling

Suppose you're at a school where students typically carry four or five three-credit courses per term. Using the advice above, you've identified five courses you would like to take. What's the next step? At this point it is important to consider when the courses you want will be given. Obviously, you can't take two courses offered at exactly the same time, and you should allow yourself some time during the day for lunch or a break if at all possible.

Fortunately, many courses are offered in multiple sections—the same course taught at different times by different instructors. In planning your schedule, take into account any commitments you may have both on and off campus. Also, consider when you might study or go to the library. It might seem like a good idea to cram all your classes into two days a week so you can spend the other three days at the library. This doesn't work out well for most people because it is difficult to listen to four lectures in a row and to study for eight hours at a stretch. (Some suggestions on scheduling are given in Chapter 6.) Once you have the schedule that seems best for you, you have what we might call your "preferred battle plan."

Now You Must Develop Alternatives

Very few students, especially in their first semester, are able to get the schedule they have planned. When you go to **register** (sign up for your courses), you might be **closed out** of a course that you want to take. This means that the section you are interested in is full before your request has been processed. At many colleges students who have been there for previous semesters are able to **advance register** or **preregister**, and they sometimes take up all the spaces in popular courses. In this case you may have to wait until the next semester when you are a continuing student and can preregister.

Another reason you might not be able to take a course is that there may be some last minute changes in the schedule, and the course may not be offered. You might also go to the first meeting of a class and decide you're not interested in it after all.

For all these reasons you should develop a "flexible battle plan." For each course you plan to take, you should choose another course that fits into your schedule, or fits with few changes. If you build this flexibility into your original plan, you will be better able to deal with any problems that come up. There is nothing more discouraging than working on a schedule for hours, planning just exactly what you want with just exactly the right times, and then finding out you can't get into three of the courses. With alternative courses in mind, it's much easier to roll with the punches.

Visit the Bookstore

Browse through the bookstore, looking at the textbooks assigned for the courses you are considering. At this point you might want to change your plans, since the course you thought would be really exciting now looks boring after you see what you will have to read.

You might want to buy your books before classes start. The disadvantage to this is that you'll have to return them if you are closed out of a course, or you decide you don't want to take it after all. Usually, though, there is no problem returning books as long as you *don't write* in them, and you return them by a specific date. An advantage to buying your books in advance is that you will avoid going to buy a book and finding that it's been "sold out." Bookstores can run out of the texts that have been assigned for a certain course if enrollments are greater than expected. When this happens, the bookstore will usually order more books, but it may be a while before they arrive. Another advantage to getting to the bookstore early is that you may be able to save money by buying used books sold back to the bookstore by students the previous semester.

Do You Need to See an Adviser?

If you haven't already met with a counselor or adviser, now is the time to do it, especially if you are a freshman. Many colleges assign each student an **academic adviser.** The role of this person differs from college to college. In some, the adviser must approve a student's set of courses each term and sign a card or form showing the student has seen an adviser. In others, the adviser is there if you want to get a faculty member's opinion, but you are not required to go see him or her regularly. In either case, advisers may point out things you hadn't thought about or can reassure you that you are on the right track.

You should always, however, go through the steps of planning your program that we describe in this chapter *before* you see your adviser. It is a waste of the time you have with an adviser to ask him or her to read the college requirements to you. If your adviser has to spend a lot of time telling you about information you should already know, he or she will have less time to listen to, and think about, your career plans or the courses you are thinking of taking. Many students feel that faculty members aren't interested in them, or that they never just joke or chat. Sometimes, though, this is because the student has not come prepared enough to leave time for these other things.

If you are having trouble with your course work or study habits, tell your adviser about it, and you may get some helpful tips. Your academic adviser is usually not expected to help you with personal problems that are unrelated to your academic work; most campuses provide other places to go for these problems (see Chapter 8). However, if you are not sure how to get help with a personal problem, your adviser may be able to make some suggestions about where you could try.

Remember Add-Drop

An important thing to remember in choosing your courses is that you can almost always change your mind—up to a point. Find out about **add-drop** deadlines; these are dates after which you cannot add or drop courses. During the first week, many students visit more classes than they can take so they can see which ones are best. Attend as many classes as you can. This will let you collect information about what the course will cover, reading assignments, tests, etc., as well as first-hand impressions about instructors.

Write down everything the professor says the first day. Be especially sure that you get the professor's name, office hours, and room number. If you're not sure about the pronunciation of his or her name, raise your hand and ask. Use a notebook, not scraps of paper that will get lost. There are several reasons to write down as much as you can. Later when you're trying to decide which courses to keep and which to drop, you won't have to rely on your memory about specific requirements, etc. Also, you'll have the information you'll need if you decide to stay in a course. A lot of information about what the professor expects is given out the first day and may not be repeated.

3.

Faculty as People

If you are like most students, you may be curious about your professors. What are they and their lives really like outside the classroom? There is no simple answer to this question because professors are as diverse as students. Just about all profs have in common is interest and expertise in some area of study and a willingness to share their knowledge with others. Beyond that, you'll find people with two left feet and others who could be professional athletes, some who are shy and some who are outgoing, some who are interesting to be around and others who are deadly dull. Professors come in as many varieties as other people. In fact, simply remembering that they *are* people can help you.

The most useful advice we can give you for dealing with faculty is to follow the golden rule: treat them as you would like to be treated yourself—politely, honestly, humanely. Since faculty are people too, you will find that if you are nice to them, they are much more likely to be nice to you. This advice holds both in and out of class.

In Class

Most professors teach several classes each year, and if you could eavesdrop on their conversations you'd learn that they feel some classes are better than others (just as you do) and more enjoyable to teach. This depends partly on class size and topic. Some faculty prefer small classes and some large, and all faculty teach courses on favorite subjects and have those they teach because somebody has to. Over and above size and subject, though, all have had favorite classes they looked forward to and classes they went to only because it was their job. While we don't have any research on this point, we think it's likely that a professor does a better job on a class s/he likes, and that the students get more from it as well.

Why Do Faculty Like One Class Better Than Another, and How Can You Get Your Professor to Like Yours?

Suppose you taught one class where students seemed interested in, and excited by, what you said. The students asked good questions, laughed at your jokes, and turned in thought-provoking papers and exams. Suppose you taught a second class in which many students cut class, talked, read the newspaper, or slept stretched out in the back row, and where the only questions were "How long is the term paper?" and "What do we have to know for the exam?" Which group of students would you work harder for?

How can two classes with the same professor be so different? We don't know. Professors have a lot of theories—lunch time classes are bad because people are either starving or stuffed and napping; late afternoon classes are bad because everyone is tired; 8 a.m. classes are bad because neither the teacher nor the students are awake yet; classrooms with lots of windows are bad in the spring; classrooms with no windows are bad because you go to sleep. Of course, there are lots of exceptions to all these "rules." What the class is like is partly luck. Things happen in the first couple of days that make everyone like or dislike everyone else. Also, we know from experience that it's hard to turn the class around. A class in trouble after two weeks is unlikely to suddenly come to life without some effort from the people involved.

Things to Do

What can *you* do, other than suffer, if you are in such a lifeless class? Actually, there is quite a bit that even just one person can do, and even if it doesn't save the class, it can improve your own experience.

First, there are things you should do if you want the professor to feel this is a class to be excited about. Two of the most important of these are to come to class regularly and to ask good questions. Being in class tells the professor you are interested in what is going on. Good questions show you have been paying attention and have been thinking about the material. This is one of the professor's biggest rewards—to know the students are responding to what s/he said.

Good questions let the professor know which points need more discussion. Questions asked only to get attention or to show off what you know are not good ones. Personal questions (the kind that begin "When I was a kid" or "My grandmother once said") usually don't add much either. Research has shown that only about 20% of a class ask questions, and this includes the bad questions! Try to ask one good question per day and try to get a couple of friends to join you. It is even okay to ask the professor to go over complex and confusing points a second time. Professors want to know when they aren't reaching students. However, it is not wise to ask for a second run-through on something you missed because you were daydreaming or because you didn't do the assigned reading. It's unfair to the rest of the class.

There are a lot of other little things you can do to make the professor feel this class is one to get up for. You can sit near the front of the class and look alert. You can thank the professor after an especially good class and say you enjoyed it (this happens pretty rarely even to popular professors and is always appreciated). You can speak to the professor after class about an interesting point. If you are lucky you may make the professor feel the whole class is a terrific group—other students may even begin to follow your example. At the least, the professor will remember you, and you will get more out of the class. This is not apple polishing, it's just treating your professor as another human being.

Things Not to Do

There are also things you shouldn't do—things that are so incredibly rude the professor thinks s/he is talking to a bunch of boors who just aren't

worth the effort. Would you continue to talk to someone who held a newspaper between the two of you? We've never understood why anyone would pick a classroom to sleep in or to read the morning paper in, but if you do, consider how this affects the rest of the class and the professor.

Don't talk while your professor is talking. S/he is not a TV set no matter how far away. S/he's a real person who can hear you, a person with feelings and pride that can be hurt by rudeness just as you can. Come to class on time. Don't throw paper airplanes. And finally, think how you would feel if you'd spent four hours preparing a lecture and another hour giving it, and then a student who missed class came in the next day and asked, "Did you say anything important?" Do you really think the professor is going to say "No" or give you in two sentences what it took an hour to say the day before? Borrow the notes from another student and then go see the professor if you need to.

If you do all the right things and none of the wrong ones, you should have a much better class and a much better relationship with your professor. In fact, as you might have guessed, these are all rules of classroom etiquette it would pay to follow in a class that's going well. Good can always get better.

Why Bother?

Why, you might ask here, should you be the one to put in all this effort? Shouldn't the professor do it? After all, it's his or her job. True, in an ideal world the professor would teach dynamically even to a class of zombies, but college works like the rest of the world. Professors are people and have human failings, one of which is a tendency to be nicest to the people who are nicest to them. You should take charge of your life as much as you can, and this includes not simply suffering through a deadly class. Rather than just complaining to your friends about the class, try the positive approach—at the least, making the effort might make the class more interesting.

Of course, professors should observe rules of courtesy too, and they should constantly be trying to keep up high standards in teaching. They should come to class on time (just as you should) and finish on time so you will not be late for your next class. They should be organized in their lectures and clear about what the course requirements are. They should lecture about the course material and related topics and not treat you like a captive audience for their political ideas or religious views. If you have reason to feel that one of your professors is not keeping up his or her end of the bargain, go see or write a note to the department chairperson. This person has the responsibility for the overall quality of teaching in a department.

Who Are These People Called Faculty?

Most regular faculty members at institutions with graduate programs have a Ph.D. (Doctor of Philosophy) degree. The degree means that they have completed advanced course work in a field (not necessarily philosophy!) and have written a dissertation consisting of an original piece of research or scholarship. People with a Ph.D. may be addressed as "Doctor" plus their last name (e.g., Dr. Smith) but never just as "Doctor" alone unless they have a medical degree. In some colleges the use of titles is discouraged, and faculty with Ph.D.'s prefer to be addressed as civilians (e.g., Mr. Smith). In other colleges Professor Smith is what is used. You can tell which is correct by listening to how faculty refer to each other in talking with students or by paying attention to how a professor introduces him or herself. Never call faculty members by their first names unless invited to do so. Also, not all faculty members have Ph.D. degrees. If in doubt, it is safest to use the title "Professor," which is always appropriate, and for women it avoids the Miss, Mrs., or Ms. dilemma.

Faculty Ranks

Faculty members at a particular institution usually have a rank depending roughly on the amount of time they have spent there and on evaluations they have received from their colleagues. The lowest ranks are **instructor** and **lecturer** with the next highest being **assistant professor** (which does *not* mean the person is an assistant to a professor). From assistant professor, faculty members may be promoted to **associate professor** and then finally to **professor** (sometimes called "full professor"). The time between promotions and the reasons for the promotion differ widely from college to college and from department to department within a college. Unlike the Army, faculty members are not addressed by their ranks; the title "Professor" is used for everyone.

Finally, at many colleges your "faculty" member may not actually be a regular faculty member. S/he may be a graduate student supporting him/herself as a teaching assistant (see page 189 in Chapter 13 and page 211 in the Appendix). Teaching assistants (also called T.A.'s, section leaders, and similar names) are most frequently found heading lab or discussion sections of a large course, but they sometimes teach courses of their own. They are often very enthusiastic teachers, and many students find it easier to talk to them than to professors, because they are usually younger. You call T.A.'s "Mr., Mrs., Ms., or Miss Smith" or by their first name as they choose.

Promotion and Tenure

While teaching experience may be the major reason for promotion at one college, research or scholarly work may be the basis at another. The phrase "publish or perish" is one often heard among young faculty members at institutions emphasizing research. Faculty members at such colleges are expected to make the results of their research available to others in their field. This is usually done by publishing papers in specialized magazines called **journals**. In some fields, faculty publish whole books rather than individual articles in journals, and some do both.

At many colleges, **tenure** accompanies a promotion from assistant to associate professor. A person with tenure usually cannot be removed from his or her position without evidence of gross misconduct or extreme financial crisis at the college. At its best, tenure gives faculty members the freedom to talk about ideas that may be unpopular or radical without fear of being fired. It gives them the security they need to do good work. At its worst, however, a faculty member with tenure can do a barely acceptable job and still retain his or her position. But if a college has a careful selection process for giving tenure, this should be a rare occurrence.

The decision to promote an assistant professor to associate professor with tenure is usually made no later than six years after the professor starts teaching at a college. Faculty members not receiving tenure are then given a year to look for another position elsewhere, since most institutions do not allow faculty who have not received tenure to remain as assistant professors longer than seven years. Hence the phrase, "publish or perish."

What Do Faculty Do?

There is an anecdote about a senator interviewing a college president to gather information for a congressional committee. "How many hours does your average faculty member work?" the senator asked. "Twelve hours, Senator." Clearly impressed, the senator replied, "Not a bad day's work." The humor of this anecdote, of course, is that the college president was referring to the 12 hours actually spent in class each week, while the senator assumed that he meant 12 hours a day! What kind of union do faculty members have that enables them to do this?

The answer, of course, is that time spent in the classroom is only a small percentage of the total time a professor spends working. Not included in the figure quoted by the college president is the time spent reading and preparing lectures, making up exams, grading papers, and meeting with students during office hours. Faculty members also usually serve on various committees (e.g., curriculum, graduate admissions) that have a way of consuming huge amounts of time. Also, many faculty members are involved in research, writing papers or books, and teaching graduate students. Research and graduate education alone may take up more than half a professor's time.

Teaching loads (the number of credit hours taught per semester by each faculty member) can differ greatly. At some colleges known all over the world for their research, some faculty members may teach one course per year or even one every other year. More common, though, are teaching

THAT'S PROFESSOR BAKER, HE DOESN'T TEACH... OR PUBLISH... OR DO RESEARCH... BUT HE **LOOKS** VERY SCHOLARLY....

loads of two to three courses per semester. At colleges that do not expect faculty to be involved in research, the load may be four to five courses per term.

While it is certainly possible to put in a bare minimum of work and bring home a paycheck, many faculty members find themselves putting in 60, 70, and even more hours per week. You don't hear many complaints, though, about the lousy hours. The fact is that most faculty members enjoy what they do and don't see their job as one in which they have to punch a time clock. Most consider it a privilege to teach and do research in a field that has so much interest for them. Faculty positions are highly prized jobs, especially as the shrinking number of college students has caused many universities to cut back drastically on the hiring of new faculty. Competition for openings is usually very stiff.

Out of Class

Most teachers feel they have the right to lead an ordinary life outside of work hours. You may think you agree with this but check your feelings when you run into your English professor at the local disco or neighborhood bar. Aren't you just a little surprised? If so, keep it to yourself. One of the authors of this book will never forget attending a performance of a risqué play and hearing a young woman scream from the other side of the theater, "Dr. Sternglanz, what are *you* doing here!?"

It is true that most faculty members have spent many years learning what they know. This does not mean, though, that they have become less human in the process. Most of them are ordinary people with ordinary lives and pleasures. They go to singles bars and/or bowling; raise children and/or tomatoes; are good or bad dancers, all in much the same proportion as other people. While this at first may seem a little disillusioning, it may make the idea of becoming a professor yourself more appealing.

A final point on expectations: it might seem reasonable that since a person has to be fairly smart to be a professor, you can expect him or her to know more about a lot of things than most people do. Not so. Most professors know a lot about their specialty and about their hobbies but no more than other people about anything else. Don't be disappointed when your brilliant art history professor knows zilch about cars or mental health. And in particular don't take your professor's opinion as gospel in fields unrelated to his or her specialty (or even in the specialty—but there at least

it deserves serious attention). The politics of your biology professor should not necessarily impress you any more than the politics of your doctor or your bank teller.

Do Professors Have Private Lives?

Professors deserve their home lives as much as other people. *Don't* call a professor at home unless s/he has said it is okay (this rarely happens). Call his or her office number. If you must reach a professor before class, leave a message with your telephone number at the department office. Even if a professor has said it's okay to call his or her home, don't call after 9:30 at night or before 9:30 in the morning.

Can You Talk Shop if You Meet at a Party?

You know, we're sure, how doctors and lawyers feel about free cocktail party consultations. Professors usually feel the same way. If it can wait until class time, let it. Don't pick a party to get permission to skip the final. Many professors, like other people, try to leave their work at the office. Besides, you don't know if this is his or her first drink or fourth; even professors have been known to get a little high and forget what was said or who said it. Try talking about things other than his or her class that you both might be interested in (e.g., campus politics, world politics, gardening, cars). On the other hand, if you have good news about a mutual research project, s/he will probably be glad to get it.

Inviting Faculty to Social Events

Whether or not inviting faculty to social events is a good idea depends on you, the professor, your relationship, and the event. Social events with students can be enjoyable for faculty, but sometimes what may be a social event and fun to you may not be to your professor. Faculty attend a certain number of undergraduate social events as an unwritten part of their job. If you and the professor have a strictly working relationship, the professor may think of an invitation more as work than as fun no matter how you feel about it. You shouldn't feel disappointed or offended if you don't receive a return invitation from a faculty member who has spent a dinner with you discussing the requirements for a biology major.

On the other hand, if the faculty member has already taken you out for coffee or beer a few times, and you invite him or her to a St. Patrick's Day party in your dorm suite, the event is much more social in nature. The difference here is the faculty member took the lead earlier. Also, the event does not require the faculty member to work (assuming that s/he is not invited as a college-required representative or chaperone).

Professional Relationships

"That was a very nice paper, let's go out for coffee and talk about it. Okay?" Or, "Let's go out for a beer to celebrate the results of the experiment." Suppose your professor says something like this to you—what does it mean? Does it mean your professor wants to become your basketball buddy? Does it mean s/he is making a pass at you? Probably not. What it almost always means is that the professor wants to encourage a friendly *working* relationship.

We have noticed that women especially have had little experience in combining socializing (particularly with the opposite sex) with working and may be afraid that if they accept an invitation, it will lead to a pass. This fear can cut women off from important information passed on informally in social gatherings and from the valuable contacts that can help them later in their careers (the "old boy network"). Both men and women should assume that such invitations are purely professional and act accordingly—keep things on a work-oriented basis. Don't get drunk—you are not getting smashed with your friends. Becoming overly friendly or flirty will most likely embarrass your professor and you.

Many students have difficulty telling the difference between a faculty member's professional interest and encouragement in their work and a faculty member's personal friendship. They may develop a "crush" on a professor or may assume a friendship that does not exist. A helpful guideline is that if your conversations with the professor have all taken place in the classroom, hall, or office, and if they almost always concern your work, your professor is only interested in you as a student.

If you are taking a course from a professor, it is considered unethical for the professor to develop a special friendship with you because it will make it difficult for him or her to grade you objectively. Don't put your favorite professor in an awkward position by doing such things as giving presents (these could be seen as bribes). If you like a professor as a person, wait until your course is over and s/he is free to respond as a person and not as a professional before you try to start a friendship.

Romance With Faculty

You may find you are attracted to your professor or T.A., or that s/he is attracted to you, or both. As you may guess from the section on friendship with faculty, it would be quite unprofessional for a faculty member to start a romance with a student or to respond to hints from the student. This is particularly true while the student is still in the faculty member's class. We're sure you can see that it would look like favoritism, and that both other students and faculty would be suspicious of grades given under these circumstances. As discussed in Chapter 8, crushes on faculty are common and generally are not reciprocated, but even if you have some reason to think your feelings are returned, you should keep your relationship with the professor professional until the course is over.

Similarly, if you think a faculty member is romantically interested in you, and you are not interested in him or her, the most tactful line you can take is to stick to business and, if pushed, say something like, "I don't feel comfortable discussing this while I'm your student." Even faculty (or, more likely, your T.A.) occasionally lose their heads and forget their professional role long enough to ask a student out on what is clearly a date. If this happens to you, realize that your professor has stepped out of his or her role, and that you should now treat him or her as you would anyone who asked you out and whom you don't want to date. Don't be afraid to say "no" (politely). We cannot emphasize enough that it would be a mistake to date your current professor even if you want to. Any teacher who would be hurt or turned-off by your postponing a romance until your relationship is more *equal* is too immature to be interesting!

The Occasional Rotten Apple

Every school probably has one or two teachers who abuse their position in some way. With any luck you will never meet one. However, professors have been known to give controlled drugs from the lab to students, steal lab equipment for home use, demand sexual favors in return for a good grade, skip most of their classes, or come to class drunk. While it is very unlikely that you will meet a teacher like this, if you do, you have some obligation as a member of the academic community to report him or her to the head of the department (or to the dean, if the professor is the head of the department). Do it anonymously if you must.

Of course, you shouldn't take any step as serious as this unless you are *quite* sure of your facts and your interpretation, and it is often very difficult for an undergraduate to judge these matters. If you are concerned about this kind of problem, you might want to discuss it with an administrator or faculty member whom you trust, without naming names, to see whether your interpretation is correct.

One of our examples deserves a little extra discussion here because it is one a lot of students are confused about. This is the trading of sex for grades. If you are a woman who is asked outright to have sex with a professor in order to get a better grade, and this is *very* unlikely, you should say "no" at once and, to protect yourself, tell somebody what happened. We also want to urge you to report the proposition officially as soon as possible (if not immediately, at the end of the course or even after graduation). This person has probably propositioned other students, and only many accusations by many women are likely to lead to action that will protect future students.

If the memory of this incident continues to bother you, you might also want to talk it over with a counselor or someone you know and trust. You might try people at your campus women's center, the dean of women if your college has one, or your roommate, giving them as much information as makes you feel comfortable. Remember that the responsibility for what happened is the professor's; it's his problem, not yours.

At some point you may find yourself in a position in which you *feel* you are being asked to trade sex for grades, but there has been no *explicit* statement of a proposition. You just have a general feeling that your teacher is interested in more than just a student-teacher relationship. A student often thinks that if the professor makes advances, she must accept, or her grade will be hurt. Usually, this is not true. What may be happening from the teacher's point of view is that he believes you'd like to accept, because other students have accepted in the past. Or, he may have a sincere romantic interest in you (we've suggested ways to deal with this in the previous section). The faculty member has behaved unprofessionally, however, by making advances to a current student, but faculty are people, and these things do happen.

All of what we've said also applies to male students who are approached sexually, but this is much less likely. Only a small percentage of professors are female or homosexual, and of course, as with heterosexual male professors, only a very small percentage of these would consider propositioning students. Again, however, the student should not feel he is responsible for the situation. He should refuse to become involved and should report any explicit proposition about trading sex for grades.

We have used a lot of space on this issue, but not because we think this is a common problem. It is *very* rare. We've talked about it in depth only because when it does happen it can be extremely upsetting, and a student is apt to lose perspective and feel s/he has no choice but to accept.

Who Are All These People Named Dean?

It takes a great number of people to make even the smallest college run. While faculty members are the ones who have most of the day-to-day contact with students, a number of people known as administrators are in the background trying to make things go smoothly. The **administration** (as administrators as a group are known) is responsible for planning the budget, fund raising, and admissions procedures, among other things. While larger campuses have more administrators, almost all colleges have someone in the positions described below. Unfortunately, there isn't much consistency in what jobs are called.

At some campuses, the **president** is someone you see at a **convocation** (a formal gathering of students and faculty at the beginning of the year) and at graduation (sometimes called **commencement**). Often though, the president is more directly involved in the daily life of the students and is a familiar figure on campus. In all cases, the president is the one responsible for keeping the campus ticking. Budget problems, fund raising, student unrest, and faculty promotions are among the many things that concern a president. On some campuses, incidentally, the term **chancellor** is used instead of president. These schools are generally part of a multicampus system where the name "president" is used for the person heading a whole system of colleges — but sometimes these titles are the reverse!

Most campuses also have a number of **vice-presidents** or **vice-chancellors** who are responsible for more narrow areas. Of most interest to you are the areas of academic affairs and student affairs. The **vice-president for academic affairs** deals with all parts of the academic program such as approving curriculum changes and hiring faculty. The **vice-president for student affairs** is usually responsible for campus housing and extracurricular activities that are not considered part of the academic program. Each of these people in turn delegates certain responsibility to others. At this next lower level, many of these people are called **deans**. You can have a Dean of the College, who is responsible for the undergraduate curriculum, and a Dean of Students whose responsibilities include student housing, student activities, etc.

Two other people you may have heard mentioned are the **registrar** and the **bursar**. The registrar's office is responsible for all academic record keeping, including transcripts (a record of your grades) and running the registration for courses each term. The bursar's office collects tuition payments, housing payments, etc. A final term you may have not heard before is **security.** Security forces are the "campus police" who give parking tickets and are responsible for campus property and personal safety.

Briefly, these are the people who, along with faculty, students, and support staff (e.g., secretaries), make up a college. It is entirely possible for you to go through college and never meet any administrators. However, you may have a special problem and need to see one. Without knowing anything about the people at your college, our best advice to you is to remember that administrators are people who deal daily with dozens of students, many of whom seem to forget that administrators are people too. Courtesy and a pleasant manner go a long, long way when you are dealing with other people, both in college and elsewhere.

4.

Taking Courses — Who's in Charge

Most students start college with the same attitudes and skills they developed in high school. For some students, their attitudes and skills are just what is needed to succeed in college. Unfortunately, others have the kinds of attitudes and skills that lead to failure. The worst possible approach toward college is to think of it as something being pushed on you by your parents, professors, or "society." Feeling this can lead to your simply enduring college or just getting by. You can, in fact, get through many college programs with just that attitude and do quite well in some of them, but you will graduate with an A average and a D mind. Our experience is that by their senior year many students realize how self-defeating this attitude is, even if the system allowed them to "succeed." But, by senior year it's too late to go back and get the information and skills they might have acquired with a different approach.

So what is the different approach? Instead of seeing yourself at the mercy of forces acting upon you, just doing what other people want you to do, you can see yourself as the director of your own future. You can take charge and make your own choices. Often your attitude depends on the skills you have. If you feel pushed around, it might be partly because you don't know how to take charge. Most of this chapter is about skills that will help you do this.

The Most Important Thing You Can Learn in College—How to Learn

If you are going to be successful, there is hardly any career (or hobby) that doesn't involve continued learning. You will have to keep up with new facts, theories, and technical developments. You will want to increase your range of knowledge to become more useful to your employer, clients, customers, or patients. Therefore, while the facts and theories you are learning now in college are important, equally important are the insights you should gain about the learning process itself. This is perhaps the most valuable single thing you can get from college. It is what makes you more *intelligent,* rather than simply better informed.

Gaining knowledge requires many skills such as using people, library, and laboratory resources or learning how to apply scientific or aesthetic standards. Three of the most critical skills are learning how to read or listen intelligently, how to organize information in order to be able to recall it when you want to, and how to evaluate your current state of knowledge.

What to Do When You Read

Reading intelligently and actively is something a surprising number of college students have *not* yet learned to do. Many students think that learning means memorizing. To memorize they read or recite something over and over until it is very familiar, or until they can say it "by heart." Well, this activity may allow you to say it by heart, but it will not necessarily let you say it "by head." Your mind is, after all, where you want the knowledge. Your *first* job is to *understand* the material, not to memorize it. Understanding frequently involves quite a bit of mental effort. Try to think of reading and studying as more like problem solving. Think of what you are reading as the answer to a question someone else once asked. Most of the things you are learning were discovered because someone wanted to answer a question or solve a problem.

It helps in understanding to do the following things:

Get an Overview

When you first read a chapter, flip through it quickly, looking at all the headings and subheadings, pictures, tables, and graphs and glancing quickly at the first and last paragraphs. This will give you an overview or

RAPID READING.

an idea of what the chapter is about—what the author hopes to tell you. Spend a few minutes trying to figure out beforehand what the main point seems to be. Is the author's point to describe something? Is the main purpose to raise a question and to give evidence for both sides? These few minutes will help you develop some organization for the information you are about to read.

As an example, the headings from this chapter are shown in the next box. Even if you don't know very much about taking courses, you can get a good idea about the topic and organization of this chapter from simply thinking about this outline for a minute or two.

Section Headings From "Taking Courses— Who's in Charge"

The most important thing you can learn in college—how to learn

What to do when you read
- Get an overview
- Ask questions
- Take notes
- Put things in your own words
- Sort out fact from interpretation
- Try to solve it yourself
- Look up words in the dictionary
- What about underlining?
- When to read

Homework is never optional

The keys to remembering: Understanding, organization, and recall cues
- Understanding
  Understanding without really understanding
- Organization
  Select and organize
- Recall cues

What to do in class
- Search for organization
- Take notes
- Use shorthand
- Go to class

Studying for exams
- Test yourself
- Review and space it out
- Outguess the professor

Do smart people have it easier?

This is too much work!

Need more help?

Ask Questions

If you start reading with some questions in mind, you will begin to think more like the person writing the book. You should try to come up with questions that are specifically directed at what you are reading.

There are several things the headings in this chapter can tell you, and several questions they might make you ask. First, although the chapter has nine main sections, five of them are pretty straightforward (learn how to learn, do your homework, smart people, too much work, and more help), while the four others are evidently more complicated and have lots of subheadings. The complicated sections all have something in common: they are about different actions you take—reading, remembering, going to class, and studying for exams. You might ask yourself why these four sections have so many subheadings. Because the authors think they are the most important four sections? Because there are many different skills, and you need to do each well? Why is there so much more listed under "reading"? Do most students have more problems with reading than with other areas? Or is it just because reading comes first, and lots of the points, such as "put things in your own words," can be used for all four areas?

You'll also notice that several of the headings (such as "Go to class" and "Take notes") seem to give the whole message. What can the authors have to say about going to class other than just go? Maybe they have some unusual reasons for going.

Some of the other headings are not so easy. *Do* smart people have it easier? What are "recall cues" (Are they acting lines)? How can you understand without understanding? This chapter seems to have a lot fewer definitions than, say, the "Faculty as People" chapter with all those deans and chancellors and bursars, but there are still a few, such as "recall cues," to watch out for.

Finally, how does all this relate to the title, "Who's in Charge?" Of course, professors are in charge of the courses—or are they? There are several topics that cover what the student does and can do. This is probably going to be a repeat of the message that the student can change things.

General Questions

In addition, there are some questions appropriate for many types of material. See the next box.

General Questions

- What method does the author use to get the points across: Logical reasoning from evidence? Dramatic examples? Emotional appeal?

- What are the main steps in the reasoning (or story)?

- What new techniques are described?

- What are the points of disagreement or conflict with other theories or points of view?

- How is this concept (or theme, event, research finding) like others we have read about, discussed, or heard of in lecture? How is it different?

- What is unusual about this point that makes it important or interesting?

- What are the consequences if this idea is right?

- Can I think of any applications or of any similarities to other (especially everyday or familiar) situations?

Write down the questions you want to keep in mind as you read. When you finish, close your book and without looking at your notes run through these questions again. Be careful. It is easy to kid yourself into believing that you are thinking more clearly than you really are. If you can't briefly, fairly quickly, and confidently answer your questions, you need to review or perhaps reread the material. You may not have understood it.

Take Notes

As you read, take notes and try to make the organization of what you read clear from the way you arrange your notes. For example, the next box shows a "top-down" arrangement where the main topic is at the top, the major subtopics are at the next level, ideas within each subtopic are at the next level, and so on.

Notes on Taking Courses—Who's in Charge?

Learn How to Learn

Reading	Homework	Remembering	In Class	Studying	Brains?	Too Much Work	Help
Overview		Understand	Look for organization	Test self			
Notes		Organize	Notes	Space reviews			
Own words		Cues	Shorthand	Play professor			
Facts vs. interpretation			Go				
Solve first							
Dictionary							
Underline?							
When?							

You would, of course, fill in more detail as you read. For example, in the section about *homework* you learn some techniques for making homework bearable. Write a reminder (e.g., group study) of this information under homework, and so forth.

The next box shows part of a page from the middle of an art history textbook. Look at the set of notes for this page. Here the main ideas are put into categories that are useful for several chapters. If similar information is located in the same place on each page of notes, it will be easier to compare countries or time periods during a review. This approach to note-taking is especially good for courses or texts that involve comparing items that are alike, e.g., plays, tribal cultures, theories of personality.

The Golden Age of Dutch Painting[1]

Holland, proud of its hard-won freedom, became the commercial center of Europe early in the seventeenth century. The prospering nation of merchants, farmers, and seafarers quickly developed an appetite for paintings, which became as popular as movies or sports events today. There were more painters and more art collectors in Holland than in any other country.

The court of the Prince of Orange and the Dutch Reformed Church were not buyers of pictures, unlike the Regent's court and the Catholic Church in neighboring Flanders. Dutch art, therefore, was without official ties. It was private and middle-class. The faces, the surroundings, and the way of life of the Dutch people themselves—their visible world—were recorded lovingly and with great fidelity to nature. There were religious paintings, too, but these were mostly small pictures for private collectors, rather than altarpieces to be used for worship and prayer.

The boom in painting lasted only half a century or so—the Dutch merchants and farmers proved as fickle as any prince, and paid less for pictures. Even the greatest artists would suddenly find themselves out of

---

[1]H. W. Janson and S. Carman, *A Basic History of Art* (B.V., The Netherlands: Harry N. Abrams, 1971), p. 247.

favor and hard-pressed to make a living. But that half-century was one of the most important chapters in the history of painting. . . .

Hals was the leading portrait painter of Haarlem. The sitter of his *Jolly Toper*, evidently, was quite willing to oblige Hals's wish for a more informal portrait than any artist had ever painted before. Hals is even suggesting here that the scene was unposed . . .

Sample Art Notes

The Golden Age of Dutch Painting

- *Context*—Protestant, prosperous, middle-class

- *Support of art*—middle-class

- *Typical subjects*—people, faces, interactions

- *Major artists and paintings*
  Frans Hals—*Jolly Toper; Women Regents of the Old People's Home at Haarlem*

  Rembrandt—*Tobit and Anna With a Goat; Blinding of Samson; Polish Rider; Self-Portrait*

  Etc.

Put Things in Your Own Words

As you read, stop after each page or after difficult paragraphs and try to put what the author says into your own words. This will help you see that complicated statements often contain simple ideas and will let you check out whether you have understood the material. Just being able to repeat the same words back is not a good test of comprehension.

If the test will be in essay form, and you have difficulty with essays, it helps to practice writing main ideas in your own words in advance of the test. You will find that you can remember what you have written much more easily than you can remember the words in the textbook.

A sample practice essay is shown in the next box.

Sample Practice Essay on Dutch Painting

In the early 1600s Holland was a well-off business center of Europe full of merchants, farmers, and sailors. These middle-class people bought paintings, helping to create an extremely productive period in art history and probably influencing what artists painted. The art of Holland showed, for example, ordinary people and their surroundings. This contrasts some with what we learned in the last chapter about art in Flanders, which was supported by the Catholic Church. Therefore, themes were religious.

Frans Hals was a major Dutch portrait painter. His painting, *Jolly Toper*, shows the informal style: it is something like a photograph in that it catches a man in the middle of moving—half-open mouth, raised hand, tipped wine glass. In addition to the pose, the thick brush strokes make the painting look spontaneous. Etc.

It wouldn't be efficient to write out such complete notes (in sentences) for all the information you read. However, it is a good idea to do so for particularly difficult material. Also, a couple of short practice essays not only can help you evaluate how well you are learning (see Chapter 5) but can help you build up your skills and confidence for essay tests.

Sort Out Fact From Interpretation

Any chapter can usually be separated into two types of information: *facts* or evidence and *interpretation* or opinion. Sometimes it's not easy to sort these two things out, but you will be reading more intelligently and actively if you remember that both fact and interpretation are almost always there. If you are not sure, ask the professor.

Try to Solve It Yourself

Suppose you are reading about the causes of the U.S. Civil War. Before you begin, try to think of all the things that *might* have contributed to tension between the North and the South. Then, as you read, you will be supporting some ideas and rejecting others. You will have the surprise of discovering some things you didn't come up with on your own, and you will also have a sense of satisfaction when you are right. Because you have given it some thought in advance, you will take a more personal interest in the subject and will be a more active reader.

Similarly, if the text poses a question or problem, try to answer it *before* reading on. When you are told the method to apply or the answer to a problem, it often seems obvious. You may think, falsely, that you "know" how to do that kind of problem, because you could easily follow the answer in the text. However, if you try to figure it out first, you get the chance to find out that you may not know the material well enough, after all. Also, once you've struggled with something yourself for a while and then get the correct answer, you are more likely to remember the solution and to have real insight that can help you on other similar problems.

Look Up Words in the Dictionary

It isn't always worth the time to look up every unfamiliar word you come across. Often you can get the general idea from the rest of the sentence or passage. However, there are times when you will miss something very important (perhaps the whole point!) if you don't find out what a word means. Make it easy on yourself: have your dictionary handy while you read, and make a note in the margin about the meanings of the words you look up. You will gradually build a vocabulary that will make your reading easier and easier.

What About Underlining or "Highlighting"?

Underlining the most important points while you are reading helps keep your attention on the page and allows you to read more actively. You have to separate out the points to underline from those not to underline. If you're highlighting too much, you're not being selective enough. If you're only underlining a few things, either there isn't enough information in the chapter, or you are missing the information that is there. In addition to underlining, make notes in the margins to cue you to main ideas and to help you find points to review.

Underlining and margin notes, however, are *not* substitutes for taking notes. Notes such as those illustrated in the boxes will be far more useful to you in learning and passing examinations. Note-taking is more active and demands more selection and organization than underlining does. Notes are also very helpful in testing yourself before an exam. Underlining by itself will be of less aid in studying for an exam, as explained below.

When to Read

You cannot do active reading in a rush at the last minute before an exam. Therefore, read regularly as the material is covered in class or as the assignments are listed on the course outline. (See Chapter 6, "Managing Your Time.") In addition, reading relevant information just after or just before it's discussed in lecture makes both the books and the lectures easier to understand.

Homework is Never Optional

Some students are surprised that homework is assigned in college classes. Often it is called "optional" in the sense that the homework does not count toward your grade in the course. Whether or not the homework officially counts, you should *never* consider it optional. Always do it, because in the end it *will* affect your grade. The homework problems and questions are an opportunity to practice your skills. The mistakes you make and correct on homework are less likely to be made on exams.

If you find it difficult to do homework regularly by yourself, try to make it a social event. Doing homework with another student in your class may turn something that is difficult into something that is difficult but pleasant. Remember, knowing something well is much more than simply being able to stumble through it; it's being able to deal quickly with the problem, whether it's writing an essay or working out a solution. Having that kind of expertise does not come without practice, and homework can give you that practice.

The Keys to Remembering: Understanding, Organization, and Recall Cues

Understanding

In the last section we emphasized the importance of comprehending what you read. If you can't understand something, you aren't likely to remember much of it. For example, read through the passage about balloons once and then write down as much of it as you can remember.

Balloons[1]

If the balloons popped the sound wouldn't be able to carry since everything would be too far away from the correct floor. A closed window would also prevent the sound from carrying, since most buildings tend to be well insulated. Since the whole operation depends on a steady flow of electricity, a break in the middle of the wire would also cause problems. Of course, the fellow could shout, but the human voice is not loud enough to carry that far. An additional problem is that a string could break on the instrument. Then there could be no accompaniment to the message. It is clear that the best situation would involve less distance. Then there would be fewer potential problems. With face to face contact, the least number of things could go wrong.

If you are like most people, you didn't remember much. Read the passage again after looking at the picture at the end of this chapter. Once you have a context for the information, the passage will be much easier to understand, and you will remember much more of it.

The overview you get when you glance through a chapter before reading works something like the picture did for the balloon passage, as do the questions you ask yourself before you read and the related knowledge you remind yourself of. The overview, questions, and related material you already know become a context for understanding new information.

---

[1] J. D. Bransford and M. K. Johnson, "Considerations of Some Problems of Comprehension" in *Visual Information Processing,* ed. W. Chase (New York: Academic Press, 1973), pp. 392-393.

Understanding Without REALLY Understanding

Read the story, "A Walk in the Woods," before going on.

A Walk in the Woods[1]

It was 5:30 in the morning and the sun was not yet up. The man got up quietly so as not to awaken anyone and silently got dressed. It was Saturday—a day he had long been looking forward to—and he was glad it had arrived. Once outside he walked along the fence for a while until he came to the break that formed an opening. There he headed for the forest that he so loved.

Since it was spring there was lots of foliage, so the forest was quite dense. He walked for quite a while and enjoyed the view. After some time he thought he heard voices. He looked around but could not see anyone else.

The man came to a clearing in the forest. It was muddy because of the previous day's rain, and his boots sank in deeply. When he came to a little stream he walked up it for quite a while before crossing to the other side.

In front of him darted a rabbit. At first he had an urge to shoot it, but then decided to let it be.

When he finally came to the lake he found his little boat that was moored among the rushes. He had spent many childhood days fishing from this little craft, and it was still quite seaworthy. He rowed out to the little island where he and his brother had built their shack for hunting. Everything was as they had left it the last time. Once inside he took off his shirt and put on his long-loved lumber jacket. It felt much more comfortable than his other clothes, and he liked the looks much better too.

The man turned on his radio to catch a hint of what was happening in civilization and then relaxed with his pipe.

---

[1] J. D. Bransford and M. K. Johnson, "Considerations of Some Problems of Comprehension" in *Visual Information Processing*, ed. W. Chase (New York: Academic Press, 1973), pp. 417-418.

His brother should arrive shortly, and together they would follow the lakes even more deeply into the wilderness and follow trails where few men had gone before.

You probably think that you understood this story very well. You certainly didn't find it as confusing as the last one! Often students get this sense of understanding and stop there. To see that sometimes there's still *more* to understand, read "A Walk in the Woods" again, this time knowing it is about an *escaped convict.*

Now you understand more than you did before, because you know *why* the man did certain things (e.g., got up quietly, listened for voices, changed his clothes), and you realize the *implications* of certain events (e.g., the tracks left in the mud, the noise it would make if he shot the rabbit).

In this example, we can change how much you understand by just mentioning two words — escaped convict. It's not always that easy, but the principle is the same. After you read something, ask yourself: Why? What implications are there? If you can't answer these, ask yourself: What do I *need* to know to have a deeper understanding of the material?

Organization

We have stressed the importance of organizing information as you read in order to help you understand it. As it turns out, organizing not only helps you understand, it helps you recall facts, ideas, events, and logical arguments.

An important finding obtained from research conducted on memory is that something can be *very familiar* yet you won't necessarily be able to *recall* it whenever you want. Most students find this hard to believe. To convince yourself, try to draw an *accurate* floor plan of your house or apartment, putting in all of the hallways, closets, etc. Or try to recall *all* of the words of a familiar song, one that you have heard many, many times, but one that you *never* sing, for example, "White Christmas."

Similarly, if you go to lectures and read the text once or twice, material will seem more and more familiar, and you will be able to recognize terms and even some of the exact sentences used. This is often enough to do well on multiple-choice tests if the material is not highly technical. Although you might be able to remember exactly where the information was located on the page, this level of effort is *not* enough if you want to be able to *produce* or use it in a new situation. To be able to recall information or apply it, you need to do something more than just read carefully and listen with concentration.

Select and Organize

You will not be able to remember everything; so your first job is selection, deciding what is important and what isn't. You then need to organize the important pieces of information by matching up those things that go together and arriving at a name or heading for each group of related items. This is what we did for the notes on art history and this chapter. Just as it is easier to find information in a library on a topic if it is all found in one place, it is easier to remember information if you put related points together in your mind. If you are having trouble organizing some information, there is a good possibility that you don't *understand* the concepts being discussed, and that you should seek extra help from your professor. Selection and organization are skills, and, like any others, they are built with practice.

Recall Cues

Finally, once you understand some material, you must give thought to how you are going to recall it when you want to. Cues are a way of reminding yourself of each piece of information.

Psychologists have shown that one cue is only good for so much information. For example, if you tell yourself to remember all you know about Dutch painting, you might remember three to five unrelated facts from the chapter. If, however, you tell yourself to remember "Dutch painting," and this cue leads you to three ideas—"context," "subjects," and "artists,"—then each of these concepts can serve as a cue to get you to several more ideas, and so on.

Many recall devices invented or used by people who have extraordinary memories are based on just this cuing principle. Students have been inventing memory cues for years. For example, the letters in the word HOMES can cue recall of the names of the Great Lakes (Huron, Ontario, Michigan, Erie, and Superior). The invented word SOHCAHTOA is used to help remember trigonometric functions. It can be divided into three parts, SOH-CAH-TOA, with each section representing an idea and the letters in each signaling part of each idea (Sin = Opposite/Hypotenuse; Cosine = Adjacent/Hypotenuse; Tangent = Opposite/Adjacent).

Organize the information to discover its natural structure and cues. If it doesn't have a natural structure, invent cues such as arranging first letters into a word as we did above. If you understand the principle behind the making of recall cues and if you keep in mind that any one cue is limited in how much information it can bring back, you have a powerful tool for studying effectively.

What to Do in Class

Lectures usually give you one person's selection and organization of the material. They highlight what the professor thinks are the important points, developments, issues, or evidence in a field. Sometimes s/he will organize these for you into an outline on the blackboard, or s/he may follow a syllabus handed out at the beginning of the semester. Write down the outline from the board or look at your syllabus often to *remind* yourself of the organization the professor is using. It is important to go to class even if you think the professor is just "rehashing" the book, because the professor's lectures and the text may be organized differently.

Search for the Organization

Some professors make their organization of information clearer than others. In any event, *your* job is to figure out what it is. In addition, you should watch for clues that the professor thinks some information is particularly important. If it appeared in the outline, took up a lot of lecture time, was written on the blackboard, or was defined in three different ways or with five different examples, it is important. "Don't be surprised if you get questioned on this" is a dead giveaway.

Take Notes

You probably won't remember facts, the organization, or clues to what's important unless you write them down; so, you must take notes as well as go to class. Taking lecture notes is also a skill that develops with practice. When should you write, and when should you listen? You won't be able to write everything down word for word, and even if you could it wouldn't be a good idea. If the professor puts it on the blackboard, put it in your notes. Important things you are not familiar with should be written down in

detail; those facts you already know should be noted with only a word or two so you remember later that they were relevant to this lecture. Unimportant items should be left out entirely.

Use "Shorthand"

Develop your own shorthand for taking notes. Make up symbols for commonly used words; for example, "rt" for "rather than," "w" for "with." You'll find you can leave out vowels and still understand the words in context as with "prcptn" for "perception."

Another important part of successful note taking is a way of showing yourself what items go with what. It doesn't matter whether this is done as an outline or as ideas grouped on the page, just try to keep some organization going.

Another thing many people do is to put brackets ([   ]) around facts or comments that come up by chance during the lecture. For example, if the professor wanders off the topic but makes an interesting point, put his or her remarks in brackets. If a student asks a question and the answer is interesting but not on the main point of the lecture, put that in brackets too. Put your own thoughts in brackets as well. Note with some symbol, for example your own initials, where the idea came from. Later this will help you sort out the *main point* of the lecture from things that come up by chance. These notes later might give you ideas for term papers, research projects, or follow-up reading.

Don't write everything down, only the important things. If you find you have trouble reading your lecture notes later, sit down within a few hours after class and write them out in more detail.

Go to Class

For most of us, notes serve as a *reminder* of what went on in class. You won't be able to understand somebody else's notes unless s/he is a very good notetaker and uses the same symbols you do. You would not expect a snapshot from somebody else's vacation to give you a vivid idea of the experience in the same way a snapshot of your own vacation does. You had to have been there! Missing class with the idea of borrowing somebody else's notes is a big mistake. The person you borrowed the notes from may not have made the right selection of the material, may not have organized it in the same way as the professor, and may not have written down clues as to what is important and what will be on the exam. Again and again we've noticed that A students come to class, and F students are hardly ever there.

Going to class and taking good notes on the lectures are probably the most efficient study techniques. This is often the way to get the most information for the least work. Hard reading assignments are easier if you've gone to the lecture on the same topic and already know what the important points are. It will cost time later if you skip class now. In a lecture the professor is doing much of the work for you or, at the least, showing you how to do it. Take advantage of this.

You might think you can do almost as well by going to class all the time and not taking notes, but without notes you are likely to forget what happened. Taking notes requires selection and organization and changes you from a passive listener into an active student.

Studying for Exams

Test Yourself

If you have been going to class, reading regularly, and taking notes on both, most of the learning for exams has already taken place. You should be able to look at your class and text notes and remember the important points that were covered. You can also use your notes to test yourself on your memory of the material. One way to make this practice testing more like a real test is to take notes on your notes. These "mini" notes should consist of *key words* or phrases that will later serve as cues to remind you of whole topics. If you can recall the information with just a key word or two as a reminder, then you have learned the material well enough to be able to use it on an essay exam, for short answer questions, and in conversation.

You *cannot* find out if you know the information well enough by only glancing through the textbook at what you have underlined. You will not be able to tell how much of the information you are remembering and how much of it you are just seeing on the page as you glance at it. (Research has shown you see more than you think you do!) You know material well when you can come up with it when you want to, using only a few small reminders.

If you learn how to evaluate what you know by yourself, you will be much better able to direct your study time and effort to where it is needed. If you wait for the professor to make the first evaluation for you, it will be too late.

Review and Space It Out

One of the oldest facts known about memory is that the more times you review your notes by testing yourself, the longer you will remember the information. Even a single review *after* you think you know it well can dramatically increase the length of time over which you can remember something. We also know something else important: *spacing out* these review sessions is usually much better than *cramming* them all together. For example, it is better to run through that Spanish vocabulary list on three different days (for 30 minutes per day) than to run through it three times in a row (for 90 minutes on one day).

Spacing gives you a chance to forget or to become confused, and, strange as this may sound, this is good! Often things you can remember for a few minutes are not there when you want them the next day. Also, over time, we tend to become confused about similar points that once seemed very distinct. If you give yourself a chance for some of this confusion to take place, you have a better chance of clearing it up. If you see what information you hesitate on or forget entirely, you can give special attention to it. It may take time for your weaknesses to show up. What you don't want is for them to show up for the first time on an exam.

Outguess the Professor

Another good way to study for exams is to try to outguess the professor; try to figure out in advance what type of exam the professor will give. Make up questions you think the professor will ask. If the exam will be short answer, definitions, or identification questions, you should be able to write down quickly a *brief* and to-the-point description of the main terms, events, etc., from the reading and lectures. If the exam will have discussion-type questions or essays, you will have to be able to write more with fewer reminders. Essays usually cover the main points of the course. For example, you might be asked to show how the same theme appears in three different plays. If you try to decide in advance what is likely to be emphasized, it will keep you thinking, and you will find that you can *very often* correctly guess the sort of questions that will be asked.

Do Smart People Have It Easier?

A lot of people think smarter students don't have to work as hard as those who aren't as smart. This is probably the wrong way to think about it. Smart students, or students who do well, are people who already know and use most of the things discussed in this chapter. Students who are not doing well often put in lots of time, but *they are not doing the right things.* For example, they are reading the material several times, but they are not taking notes. They are not sorting out fact from interpretation. They are not organizing the material, and maybe most importantly, they are not testing themselves to find out what they know and what they don't know.

Another difference between good and poor students is good students know some material is more difficult; they don't expect every course to be easy. They learn to take brief notes when the material is easy and more detailed notes when the material is difficult. Good students also plan to spend more time in review and self-testing when the material is difficult.

Many students fail not because they don't try, but because they don't know how to play the game. You wouldn't play tennis without learning the rules and trying to develop a higher and higher level of skill. Why spend four years (and sometimes more) at something without trying to get better at it?

This Is Too Much Work!

Isn't all this a lot more work? It probably is somewhat more work (but probably not *that* much more considering the "all nighters" you can skip with this system). However, the work is spread in small doses over a whole term; so, it won't seem that bad. The question really is will the little extra work and this *new style* of working pay off? If you are a long-time procrastinator and last-minute crammer and can't bring yourself to make a total change all at once, you might try using our system in just one course (your most important) at first. If you follow our suggestions carefully, we are sure it will show up in your grade and in your attitude toward the course. Not only that, we know from memory research that using our system increases the likelihood of your remembering much of what you've learned long after the course is over.

Need More Help?

If you need more detailed help than we can provide here, there are several books listed at the end of the chapter that you might find useful.

Also, your college may have a learning center or a noncredit study skills course. Either of these will give you instruction in how to study, sometimes tailored for the particular courses you are having trouble with. Take advantage of these opportunities if you need to. What you learn in college about how to understand and remember information (and how to express what you know—see the next chapter) is a skill that will be useful for the rest of your life.

Suggested Readings

Froe, O. D., and Froe, O. B. *The Easy Way to Better Grades.* New York: Arco Publishing, Inc., 1959.

Maddox, H. *How to Study.* New York: Fawcett Premier Books, 1978.

McKowen, C. *Get Your A Out of College: Mastering the hidden rules of the game.* Los Altos, CA: William Kaufmann, Inc., 1979.

Richard, J. A. *A Student's Guide to Better Grades.* North Hollywood, CA: Wilshire Book Co., 1964.

Robinson, F. P. *Effective Study.* 4th ed. New York: Harper & Row, 1970.

Shaw, H. *30 Ways to Improve Your Grades.* New York: McGraw-Hill Book Co., 1976.

Smith, S., et al. *Best Methods of Study.* New York: Harper & Row, 1970.

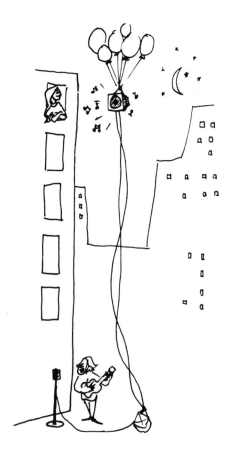

5.

Showing What You Know

Many students believe that if you're simply interested in material and concentrate on it, you will learn. In the last chapter we tried to convince you that interest and concentration are not enough. In order to *understand,* you have to actively try to tie one point to another as well as to what you already know. If you don't know how to organize information and to evaluate what you know by testing yourself, you will have a difficult time remembering.

Many students also believe that whether or not they do well on tests depends on whether they're tired, distracted, anxious, or under personal stress in their life. These things may affect how well you do, but much more important is how well you know the material in the first place. The better you know something, the more stress it takes to make you forget it. Just ask any pilot, surgeon, or actor.

Taking Tests

If you follow our advice on studying, you should do well on tests and in other situations in which you must use what you have learned. In addition, there are some things you can do while you are taking tests that should help you show what you know.

Multiple-Choice Questions

Be sure to read carefully each question and the alternative answers. This seems obvious, but many students stop reading carefully as soon as they find something that seems to fit the question, and they miss the better answer. One thing to do when you don't know the answer is to rule out answers that are clearly wrong. If there are four alternatives for a question, you may be able to rule out two of them, and this will double your chances of getting the answer right. The boxes on "Syphilis and Pregnancy" and "The Law of Diminishing Returns" illustrate how to rule out alternatives in answering multiple-choice questions.

Syphilis and Pregnancy

Suppose you learned in class that if a pregnant woman with syphilis is treated by the fifth month of pregnancy, her baby will not be harmed by the disease. If she goes untreated until later in the pregnancy, however, the baby will be affected. A question based on this information might read:

Which of the dates below is the latest at which a pregnant woman may be treated for syphilis without risking harm to the fetus?

   a. first month

   b. third month

   c. seventh month

   d. ninth month

You may feel that this question should include fourth or fifth month to be fair but read it again. Can she be treated safely in the seventh month? No. In the ninth month? No. In the first month? Yes. In the third month? Yes. Which is later, first or third? Many questions are written like this so the professor can see if you know more than just a connection between the words "fifth month" and "syphilis."

The Law of Diminishing Returns

Some multiple choice questions can be quite difficult. A chapter in an economics text might include a discussion of the *law of diminishing returns*. This law describes a relation between an input to production (such as labor) and the output or product (such as corn). If one laborer works a field and can produce 2000 bushels of corn, how many bushels can two laborers produce working the same field? Three laborers? According to the law of diminishing returns, each new unit of input (laborer) adds less and less to output (bushels of corn), *assuming other inputs* (such as amount of land) *stay the same.* Here is a multiple-choice question based on this information:

According to the law of diminishing returns:

   a. If you double the number of guns you want, you will have to give up some butter.

   b. If you double labor and land, you will only add about 50% increase in production of apples.

   c. If you double labor and hold land constant, you will need more equipment to produce as much corn.

   d. If you double labor and hold land constant, you will not double production of apples.

   e. If you double the number of guns you produce, you will be able to have something less than double the amount of butter.

You can rule out alternatives *a* and *e* because guns and butter are both products (output), and the law of diminishing returns relates inputs to outputs. Similarly, *c* can be eliminated because equipment is not a product. This leaves you deciding between *b* and *d*. The correct answer is *d* because it specifies that labor increases while land stays fixed.

Short Answer Questions

Read the question carefully and keep your answer short and to the point. You won't get more credit (and may *lose* some) for writing a lot of information that has nothing to do with the question. When you are identifying or defining something, it's a good idea to use an example or piece of evidence, as well as the definition. You can help say what something *is* by saying what it isn't — contrast it briefly with an alternative. For example, it may help you to describe what a "Republican" viewpoint is by showing how it is different from a "Democratic" viewpoint. If a question is worth three points, think about how you would assign these points to your answer if you were the grader. In all cases, though, make sure what you write answers the question that was asked. For an example of a short answer question, see Question 1 in the box called "Answer All Parts of the Question."

For both multiple-choice and short answer exams, answer the questions in order, don't spend too much time on any one question, and go back to the ones you skipped after you finish the others.

Essay Questions

With math problems, essay questions, or similar problems, it is very important to pace yourself properly. The first thing to do is quickly read through the whole exam, so you will have a feeling for how many questions there are and which ones will be hard and which easy for you to answer. Dividing your time wisely is an important skill on these exams. For example, if you know the answers to all the questions, start with the questions worth the most points first, leaving the shorter ones for last. If you need to write quickly at the end because you are running out of time, it will be easier if you are writing less complicated answers.

On the other hand, suppose you read through the exam, and at first it all looks impossible. At this point, it helps if you know how to *fight panic*. People panic when they don't think there is anything they can do; it goes away when they start doing something useful. If you feel yourself getting very anxious during an exam, take the question you think you can say *something* (anything) about and start organizing and writing your answer. The panic will usually disappear as you get involved in answering the question.

In addition to helping you divide your time, reading quickly through an exam before you begin will help you in another way: the test questions will start reminding you of things you have forgotten. By the time you have answered one question and gone on to another, the second one may not seem so difficult. Of course, no reminder will work for information you haven't learned in the first place (see Chapter 4 on how to study).

Essay Essentials

In essays, try to *define* any special terms you're using at the beginning of your answer; then, if appropriate, *compare* or *contrast* one idea or point of view with another. Students often present one theory as fact or one position as gospel, without even hinting that there is another side to the issue.

After you have given other people's ideas, move on to your own if this is asked for. The professor will be much more interested in your opinion *after* you've shown you know what was covered in the lectures and the text. You may not get credit for original ideas if that's all you have in your answer.

Sample essays, along with comments, are shown in the boxes called "Phenotypes and Genotypes" and "Is There Intelligent Life on Earth?"

Phenotypes and Genotypes

If you were a grader how many points out of 10 would you give each of these answers? What's wrong with each?

Question: Why isn't the genotype obvious from the phenotype alone?

Answer A: The phenotype is the way the plant or animal looks. The genotype is the actual genes the plant or animal has. They might not be the same; the animal might not look the same as the genotype because the genotype might be mixed—have two different genes. You might have genes for blue eyes and brown eyes, and brown eyes always wins.

(Generally okay. Confused "alleles" with "genes." Should have used and explained terms "dominant" and "recessive" although seems to have the right general idea. Makes the grader guess too much about what the student knows.) 6 points.

Answer B: The phenotype is the way the organism expresses the gene. If you have genes for blue eyes, they will be expressed in your eye color. The genotype is the genetic information that decides what the phenotype will be. In higher organisms there are usually two forms or alleles for each gene (there are often more than two possible different ones but only two in each particular organism). You might have eye color gene alleles for brown and blue eyes—other people might have them for green and brown, or grey and blue. Of the two alleles, one is usually dominant over the other and is expressed or comes out in the organism so you can see it; so the dominant allele decides the phenotype.

(Excellent. Both used and defined terms correctly and gave examples. This person really seems to know the material.) 10 points.

It is possible that both students felt they had a good idea of the relationship of phenotype and genotype, but only one really showed all s/he knew.

Is There Intelligent Life on Earth?

In your Astronomy 101 class you are given the following short essay question. If you were the grader, how many points out of a possible 10 would you give each of these answers?

Question: In the mid-1960s a young astronomer caused a stir by saying that if Martians examined Earth the way we had been exploring Mars, the Martians would conclude there was no evidence for intelligent life on Earth. Do you think this statement was justified at the time? Why?

Answer A: No. They could see our activities and pick up our TV reports.

(Wrong. Their instruments could not have picked up cities and TV.) 0 points.

Answer B: I think there is life on other planets. You can't dismiss the UFO reports. Besides with all the stars and planets in the universe, as we said in class, the chances are there is life on other planets somewhere.

(This student has picked up on the implication of the question [Is there life on Mars?] but did not answer the question at all. Brought in other facts but nothing relevant.) 0 points.

Answer C: Yes, it was. We were orbiting probes too far away and with the wrong measuring devices to pick up signs of our type of civilization on Mars.

(Good. Answered question; got all main points.) 8 points.

Answer D: Yes and no, mostly yes. There were a few things the Martians could have seen from as far away as our probes were from Mars at the time; these might have made them think there was intelligent life here. Intelligent life would probably make artificial changes in the environment—like the wide logging patterns in northeastern Canada they could have seen. But most such changes are too small to be picked up by the instruments in use at that time.

(Excellent. Gave both sides of question yet made a decision. Included all evidence discussed in class.) 10 points.

The "Kitchen Sink" Essay

A poor student will often write a lot but say very little. This takes time away from other questions you might be able to answer better, and you won't necessarily get very many points for the time you have spent. You may even lose points if the grader gets mad at having to wade through an empty, wordy answer. Some students try the "kitchen sink" approach—they throw in everything they can think of whether or not the question asks for it. Graders don't like this either.

Neatness Counts

Write neatly. It makes your paper easier to read, and the grader has to know what's there in order to give points. The first impression your paper makes will sometimes affect your grade. Professors, like all people, can't help but be influenced by the way you present yourself and your work. Use a pen with either blue or black ink, *never* red or green. Neatly cross out information when you change your mind. For math problems, use a dark but not soft pencil and do your work, showing all steps, in order across or down the page. Even if your answer is wrong, you might get partial credit if the grader can see what you've done. Maybe you only made a multiplication error, but the grader can't know this if there is no clue as to how you got your answer.

Check It Again

Finally, when you think you're done with a question, read it again and see if you answered *all parts* of it, as illustrated in the following box. You'd be amazed at how often even students who know the answers get involved in answering the first half of an essay question and forget, or never notice, the second half.

ALWAYS BRING A FULL PEN FOR TESTS...

AND NEVER, EVER BRING A FOUNTAIN PEN!

Answer All Parts of the Question

When you are tense about an exam it is easy to overlook part of a question. Can you see what the student overlooked in these answers?

(1) *Question:* Define two of the following three terms and give examples of each. Sedimentary, metamorphic, and igneous rock.

Answer: Igneous rock is rock that has been melted, usually in a volcano. Pumice. Tuff. Sedimentary rock is rock that was laid down as layers of sediment, usually under water.

(The student forgot to answer the whole question. S/he left out examples of sedimentary rock.)

(2) *Question:* Do you think having Klinefelter's syndrome causes people to become criminals? Define your terms. Discuss the evidence and possible interpretations, making it clear where you stand on this issue.

Answer: Just because a few people have found more Klinefelter's people in jail than you might expect doesn't mean the syndrome causes people to be criminals. It might do other things, too, like make them stupid, so that if they are criminals they get caught. It makes them tall so maybe they get used to having their way by pushing people around—but that does not mean they will all be criminals. It makes them unusual looking in other ways, too, so they might get teased and turn against society.

(The student did not define terms such as "Klinefelter's syndrome" or "criminals." The answer could use some reorganization with definitions first, then evidence, interpretation, and finally opinion.)

Still Have a Problem?

If you thought you did all this, and you still did not do well on the first essay exam, ask your professor to read aloud in class or hand out an example of a good answer (see the section in Chapter 7 about learning from a bad grade).

How to Write a Term Paper

For many students, the thought of writing a term paper is about as appealing as poison ivy or the plague. Whether or not this describes you, you will very likely have to write several papers during your years in college. There are some simple guidelines you can follow that will make writing papers less painful and maybe even enjoyable.

Professors assign papers so students can explore one topic in depth and pull together what they have learned. Papers also give you a chance to practice writing, a skill that is more important for your future than you may realize. Writing well is something you can learn to do, something that can greatly improve your chances for success in many types of jobs (even those in which the only writing you do is a memo to the boss).

Plan to take a few courses that require papers. Papers are more likely to be assigned in some classes than in others. (It is hard to imagine what a term paper on some topics—calculus, for example—would look like.) They are most common in smaller classes. The reason is simple: you may have to write only one paper, but your professor has to read and comment on all of them.

Picking a Topic

The first thing you have to do when writing a paper is to decide on a topic. Sometimes the professor will give you a lot of freedom in your selection and say, "Anything related to the course material is okay." Often the area will be narrowed down for you, and sometimes a specific topic is assigned. Usually, though, you have some choice. The best advice is to write on a topic that interests you. However, don't be discouraged if you are assigned a topic that doesn't sound intriguing at first. You would be surprised at the subjects you could like after you've written about them for a while.

Look through your notes and your textbook for possible ideas. The most important thing at this point is to choose a topic of the right size—neither too general (you will be writing forever or else very superficially) nor too narrow (it may be hard to find references). Common sense will give you some idea of whether your topic is about the right size, but often it is hard to tell for certain without first doing some library research to see how large your topic really is.

When you have a pretty good idea of what you want to write about, it's usually worthwhile to check out your topic with your professor. Stop by during office hours for a brief chat. You may be able to get some good references or may be saved from spending valuable time working on a topic that looks good at first but may give you big problems later. If possible, have a second choice in mind.

Checking Out the Library

If you don't yet know your way around the library, now is the time to check it out. Even small college libraries have much more in them than the community libraries you may be used to. Not only do they have more books and scholarly journals, they also have many more ways to help you find what you need.

Your textbook is a good place to start your research. The **bibliography** (list of references) at the back may be able to direct you to other books having useful information about your topic. The library's **subject card catalog** is useful if the name of your topic is the same as the subject heading. If not, you may have to search through the listings for a subject heading that is related or more general. This will eventually get you to the same place, but it will take a little more time. The librarian may be able to help you with this.

Never just use the first book you find to do your paper. While you certainly don't have to read every book from cover to cover, read the relevant parts of several different ones. Remember that books are like almost everything else—there are good ones and bad ones. A good book is one that presents ideas accurately and clearly and separates the author's own ideas from what is generally accepted as fact. You usually have to look at a few books to find the best ones.

For some topics, the publication date of your books is very important. A book published in 1955, for example, would be of little value to you if you are writing a paper on modern developments in genetics. The field of genetics changes so fast that even a book published in 1975 might be out of date. Here you can use the help of a **reference librarian** in finding more recent sources. **Reviews** of recent findings are published each year in many scientific fields, and your librarian will be able to show you how to find them.

The librarian can also help you find journal articles that are recent and relevant to your topic. A **journal** is a magazine (although you'll never see most of them in a drug store) that publishes scholarly work; they are subscribed to by scholars and libraries and are generally serious reading. They are the way researchers and scholars communicate with each other. *Scientific American* is a journal written by experts especially for laymen and "outsiders," but most journals are written for "insiders" and cover only a small topic, for example, *Cell Biology, Aristotelian Society Proceedings,* or *Sex Roles*. Getting information will be much easier, and you will find much more if you learn how to find and read the journals in relevant fields.

Finding References

To help researchers find articles on particular topics, many fields have books called **indexes** that allow you to look up all recently published papers on a certain topic (e.g., *Psychological Abstracts*). Some libraries even have computer terminals that allow you, together with a librarian, to rapidly search through thousands of recent articles for the ones likely to be of use to you. Find out about the resources at your own library. Talk to the librarians. Most know a lot and are extremely helpful—their job is to help people find what they need.

Organizing and Revising

After finding articles and books on your topic and reading them, your next step is to work out what you want to say in your paper. While all papers aren't the same, most can be divided into sections that introduce the topic, present relevant information, and then draw conclusions and/or summarize. A good paper presents only a few ideas, but it presents them well. Some people find it helpful to work from an outline; others find it easier to begin writing right away. Whether or not you have a formal outline, though, it's important for you to plan and organize what you want to say. If you can't make a clear outline from your paper *after* you have written it, it probably needs more work.

After you've written your paper, it's a good idea to put it aside for a day or two and then look it over again with an eye toward making small improvements. Sometimes it's hard to see problems when you have been working on a paper. Time away from it may help you see how clearly your paper reads. Give your paper to a friend to criticize. If your friend can't understand it (or if you can't yourself two days after you wrote it), your professor probably won't be able to either.

Needless to say, you can do these things only if you finish your paper well in advance of the due date. While it may seem like easy advice to give and next to impossible advice to take, the most important thing we can recommend is to start working on your papers early. The books you need will be in the library, you will have time to choose a topic of just the right size, and you will be able to go over one or more drafts of your paper.

Finishing Touches

The rules you should be following in typing your paper depend on the topic. In some fields, it's usual to give credit for the words and ideas of others with **footnotes**. In other fields, you give the person's name and date of publication right in the paper itself and list complete references at the end in the bibliography. Don't assume one way of doing a paper is correct for all subjects. If you are not sure, ask your professor which style is preferred.

No matter what style is used, though, scholars in all fields agree it is dishonest to use the work or words of others without saying so (a form of cheating called **plagiarism**). It is your responsibility to avoid plagiarizing a work. Even if you think you know what plagiarism is, read pages 76–77 in this chapter. We have known a number of students who have gotten into serious trouble because they didn't have a complete understanding of how and when to give credit to others.

We have some final words to say about the "cosmetics" of paper writing. If at all possible, type your paper on good quality typing paper, using black ink in a standard typeface. Do not use a script typeface. KO-REC-TYPE® is a terrific invention that gets rid of the need for erasable paper,

something most college professors hate because of the way it smudges. As we have said earlier, professors are people and can't help but be affected by the appearance of what you turn in. A neat, clean paper whose pages are stapled together makes a much better first impression than a sloppy, hard-to-read one that looks like it was thrown together an hour before class.

No amount of "cosmetics" will make up for a poorly researched and written paper. However, if a paper looks like it was put together by a four-year-old, the reader is likely to expect a four-year-old's thoughts.

A Sample Paper

Suppose you have to write a library paper for your anthropology course and are given a fair amount of choice about the topic. You are only in the course to fill a requirement and are having trouble getting excited about the subject of your paper. One solution is to tie the course material in with some other interest you have. For example, maybe you are not interested in old bones of prehistoric people such as the Neanderthals, but you are excited by the idea that creatures, such as Bigfoot or the Loch Ness Monster, might exist today. You could combine what you've learned in your anthropology class with your own interest.

The introductory paragraph of such a paper might look something like that in the box titled "Is Bigfoot a Neanderthal?" (Of course, you should check with your professor to be sure your topic is acceptable.)

Is Bigfoot a Neanderthal?

Introductory Paragraph

The superficial similarities between *Homo neanderthalis* and reported sightings of Bigfoot and similar creatures are great enough to raise the suspicion that the two organisms may be related or identical. Physical anthropologists have developed sets of physical and cultural criteria to settle questions of similarity between extinct species of man. These same criteria, such as tool use and foot shape, can be used to decide what the relationship, if any, of Bigfoot and Neanderthal man may be.

In general, it helps the reader if your introductory paragraph states the theme, purpose, or what you hope to accomplish with the paper.

As we said earlier, your paper will be improved if it follows an outline—made either before or after you write the paper. An outline helps you group your points and provides ideas for headings to help the reader see your organization. A sample outline for "Is Bigfoot a Neanderthal?" is given in the next box. Be sure to include parallelisms, i.e., things that share the same pattern (IVA 1, 2, 3, 4, 5 are similar to IVB 1, 2, 3, 4, 5) where appropriate.

Is Bigfoot a Neanderthal?

Outline

I.   Introduction

II. Definitions

    A. Neanderthal
       1. Dating and discovery
       2. Culture
          a. Tools
          b. Burials
          c. Group living
          d. Decoration
       3. Disappearance
       4. Conflict with Homo sapiens

    B. Bigfoot
       1. Distribution of sightings, e.g., Abominable Snowman
       2. Reports of culture
          a. Tools
          b. Group living
          c. Decoration
          d. Language

III. Basis for decisions on same or different species

    A. Living species
       1. Interbreeding
       2. Fertility
       3. Serum tests

    B. **Extinct forms of man**
      1. Teeth
      2. Bones, especially leg, pelvis, and foot
      3. Brain size
      4. Head shape

IV. **Physical similarities of Bigfoot and Neanderthal**
    A. **Neanderthal description**
      1. Size
      2. Brain size
      3. Posture
      4. Feet
      5. Skin-fur issue
    B. **Bigfoot**
      1. Size
      2. Brain size
      3. Posture
      4. Footprints
      5. Fur

V. **Conclusion**

Seminars

Most students have never been in a seminar before they get to college. Both the way you learn and the way you demonstrate your knowledge are different in a seminar than in a regular class. Once they try a seminar, many students like them better than lecture classes, but you need special skills for seminars. Learning these skills will help you enjoy seminars more, as well as do better in them.

How Are Seminars Different?

Many students avoid signing up for seminars because they don't know what they are or they sound "hard." A seminar is a small group of students (and a professor) who meet to help each other learn about some topic that is of interest to all of them. Often the students split the responsibility for covering different parts of the topic. Each person might write a paper on his or her subtopic and give it to the others to read or might talk about it to the group. In other seminars, everyone reads the same material each week and comes to class prepared to discuss and criticize it.

In a standard classroom/lecture situation, you are only concerned with your own goals. A seminar is different because each student makes a commitment to the others in the group. This includes sharing your thoughts and taking criticism well. It also means being enthusiastic about other people's ideas and being able to give them helpful criticism. If there is an assignment to be read before class, you should *think about it* as well as read it. It will be clear to everyone if you haven't given the reading much thought. The most successful seminars are those in which everybody feels a responsibility to the other people.

What Do Professors Look For?

Seminar professors differ but most look for the same types of things. In written assignments, they like to see ideas presented clearly. They also want to see some signs that you have done the readings. If you are asked to lead a discussion, you should answer other people's comments, and you should not be defensive if your ideas are criticized.

Most students are very anxious about having to lead a discussion or give a presentation for the first time. This is natural. If you are nervous at the start, keep talking; the nervousness will go away. Many students find they actually enjoy talking to the class once they discover that people are genuinely interested in what they have to say and are not looking for flaws in their appearance or style of expression. If you have a time limit on your presentation, practice it to see how long it will take. You will be amazed at how fast the time goes, especially if you allow for questions or other interruptions. This way you won't be trying to squeeze everything into the last two minutes. Rehearse out loud by yourself or in front of friends if you are especially nervous. The more you have done something, the easier it is.

Attendance is often optional in lecture courses, but it is required in seminars. It is particularly rude to miss class when another student is leading a discussion or presenting his or her ideas. If you have to be absent, you should let the professor and the student leading the discussion know why. Be sure to pick up the assignment for the next meeting. If you don't, you will really be missing two classes since you won't be able to participate well in the next discussion without having read the assignment.

Remember, the important difference between a seminar and a regular class is the amount of responsibility you, the student, have in running the class.

Cheating

Bringing notes into an exam when they are not allowed, copying answers from another student on an in-class or take-home exam, and working with others on a project you're supposed to do by yourself are all forms of cheating. We're sure you've heard of others.

One form of cheating that causes some confusion is **plagiarism.** Plagiarizing is taking the work of others and trying to pass it off as your own. Using a term paper written by another student (or buying one) is a form of plagiarism, as is copying a chapter from a book or an encyclopedia and turning it in as your own work. Of course, you can use other people's work as a starting point, but you must make clear what has been borrowed and what is your own.

There are rules for doing this. A basic rule might be "never copy a whole sentence of someone else's work without giving them credit or rephrasing it in your own words." In addition, you should never try to pass someone else's ideas off as your own. No matter how you rephrase someone's ideas, the person who came up with them deserves the credit. *You* will get credit for having found the idea.

Rules may vary slightly from campus to campus; they may not be the same ones you used in high school. It is your job to really understand them. Your professors expect that you know the rules, and they will probably not explain them to each class. If you have doubts about whether something is "legal," ask the professor before you turn in your paper.

Why Do Students Cheat?

It's rare that plagiarism or cheating is "accidental." It usually happens because someone thinks there is no alternative. Most students who cheat are overwhelmed by pressure and fear. You may be afraid that you're not going to have a high enough grade point average to get into medical school, or that you'll be thrown out if you fail one more course. You may be worried that if you don't get at least a B you'll lose face with your parents or your friends or possibly lose your scholarship. You might think that if you don't turn your paper in before the spring vacation, you'll have to write it over the holiday and miss a Caribbean cruise. A pressure that may not seem very important to someone else may still make the person involved feel trapped.

There are a lot of pressures at college. For many students it's the first time they've really had to plan how to spend all of their time. It's the first chance they've had to decide what's most important. You may choose to put friends ahead of work, or you may choose to put your efforts into one course rather than another. Whenever you make choices, though, there are costs. Ideally, once you've made the choices, you learn to live gracefully with the results.

There Must Be a Better Way

All of us tend to panic a little sometimes when we're faced with the results of our earlier choices. Some students are tempted to cheat because they can't pass the course (with the grade they want) in any other way. If you find yourself so overwhelmed by the pressure that you are tempted to cheat, discuss the situation with the professor. You might be able to work out an extension on a paper deadline or get some help with a plan to catch up.

At the worst, you may have to get a bad grade in the course, but remember, even then you are not stuck with it. In most colleges you may repeat a course even if you did not actually fail it the first time (perhaps in summer school or at night during the summer at a community college). It will not count twice toward graduation, of course, and your grade point will be based on some kind of average of the two courses, but this may be better than leaving a D in an important course on your record. Graduate schools and employers will be more interested in whether you ever learned statistics than in how many times you took it. Another thing to consider is that later on you may have to use what you didn't learn if you cheated.

Whatever your reason for being tempted to cheat, there are more reasons not to cheat. Students who copy some answers from a student sitting next to them simply to gain a few points risk a great deal for very little. If you are caught, it will be *much worse* for your record than any bad grade. In many colleges you can be dismissed (expelled or suspended) for even a first offense. You will hurt your reputation among the faculty and your friends. People will doubt the worth of your other good grades. Even if you were never officially caught, if people know or suspect that you cheated, this will influence their feelings about you. Your friends may joke about it in college, but they'll remember it later when they're asked to recommend someone for a job.

Most importantly, you have your own character to consider. This is the time of your life when you are deciding who you are and what you stand for, what your strong and weak points are. You can't build self-confidence about your ability to handle things by cheating. Some corner of your mind will suspect that you can't make it without cheating. You will feel better about yourself if you face up to the results of your poor study habits, heavy partying, or academic weaknesses and do something useful to get out of the mess and prevent its ever happening again.

6.

Managing Your Time

It's halfway through the semester. You have been going to classes fairly regularly and doing the reading for the class you find most interesting, but now you are beginning to worry about midterm exams. You get up one morning feeling good and decide today is the day to "catch up on everything." So you decide to skip the one afternoon class you have (you can get the notes from a friend) and settle down for a day's work on the couch in the lounge.

Just then your roommate comes along and tells you about a terrific new movie (25 minutes). A few minutes later someone else convinces you to sign a petition (10 minutes). Soon after, an article in the newspaper on the coffee table catches your eye, because it seems related to the petition you just signed (five minutes). Since you're already looking at it, you decide to browse through the rest of the newspaper (40 minutes). Finally, you force yourself to get back to the problem at hand and make a list of what you have to read, the notes you have to review, and other assignments due before midterms.

When you see how much it adds up to, you begin to panic. You pick up one book and start to read, but you find yourself worrying about the other things you have to do. You switch to a different book and then a third. As the day goes on, you feel more and more frustrated because it becomes obvious that you aren't going to even come close to finishing *everything*. That night you realize just how awful the situation is. You wake up the next morning with a stomachache and spend the whole day reading magazines. Then you feel even worse, because now you are further behind than ever. Besides, if you were going to goof off for a whole day, you'd really rather have gone to the beach or to that movie everyone is talking about.

Sound familiar? This is the sort of thing that happens to everybody now and again. Unfortunately, it happens to quite a few people a lot of the time.

Goals

One reason people don't get much done is that they actually haven't decided to do anything. They have some vague wishes, but they don't have any goals. There are three kinds of goals you should think about, and they are all related to each other: long-range goals (say, five years from now), medium-range goals (for the semester or quarter), and short-range goals (this week and today).

Long-Range Goals

For example, some long-range goals might be to be accepted into graduate school if you decide to go; to have a job in advertising, social services, or publishing; to be in a bank's management training program; to be a carpenter; to write a book of poems. Of course, you should have personal goals as well as career goals. Some long-range personal goals might be to be an educated person; to make some contribution to society through volunteer work or social action; to find someone to love; to participate in sports. Try it. What are your long-range goals? Write them down. Be as specific as possible, realizing that they may change or that maybe you can be more specific next year.

Now, try to see what you are doing in college in relation to these long-term goals. Hopefully, you are selecting your courses and major with your own career and personal goals in mind (see Chapter 13). The courses you take will help you reach your goals by giving you information, ideas, and skills you might need. The level of your performance also will determine, in some cases, whether or not you will get the chance to pursue your long-range goals.

Medium-Range Goals

With your long-range goals in mind, you should write down a set of medium-range goals at the beginning of each semester or quarter. These will depend on your particular situation, and no one else can set them for you. Here are some examples from four different people to help you get the idea:

Medium-Range Goals

- Get straight A's
- Learn tennis
- Write applications to graduate schools

- Get four B's and one C
- Lose seven pounds

- Get three B's and two C's
- Write three poems
- Quit smoking
- Make one new friend

- **Get all B's**
- **Join and participate in a political action group**
- **Get information about potential careers in advertising**
- **Save $200**

When you first make your list, there might be 10 or 12 goals on it. Choose no more than four and write them down according to how important they are to you right now. Save the others for later; you can only do so much in a single term.

As you can see from the examples, one of your goals should be a specific statement about how well you want to do in your classes. This should depend on your long-range goals, your current level of study skills (see Chapters 4 and 5), and your past performance. You may want to be an A student, but last semester you got all D's. Be realistic. You are not likely to improve that dramatically in one semester. Always set goals that are a challenge but are within reason. If you do not care much about grades as long as you pass, be open about this with yourself. Write down that you expect all C's. Students who could do better but don't are sometimes disappointed at the end of the semester. But if you have been honest with yourself about your expectations and how much effort you are willing to put in, you shouldn't be disappointed.

Short-Range Goals

Some short-range goals for the week might be to finish the practice problems at the end of Chapter 7 for calculus, to read *Long Day's Journey into Night* for your American theater course, or to go to one social event on campus. Some short-range goals for a particular day might be to do the first practice problem in Chapter 7, to read the first act of the play, to do your laundry, or to pick up a campus newspaper.

Developing a Plan

Now you have to figure out a way to reach your goals. You will need a plan. We will concentrate on plans for reaching academic goals, but much of what we suggest works for personal goals as well. The first thing to realize is that vowing to "work hard for the whole semester" is not a plan, nor is deciding to "cut down on social life." These are vague promises to yourself that are very hard to keep. Deciding to "keep up with the work each week and not fall behind" is a bit better but still not specific enough to do you much good.

Being a student is much like being a high-level executive. You have to budget or divide up your time for various difficult tasks. You have to decide which things are most important (develop priorities), and you often have to come up with a way to attack problems. You have to pull together information from many sources, meet deadlines, create solutions to problems, write reports. You are constantly being evaluated. How well you do depends not just on your intelligence or abilities but on your judgment. Did you spend your time wisely? Did you work efficiently?

A plan requires that you consider *Where, When,* and *Exactly What* you are going to do.

Where (Managing the Environment)

Whether or not you are hungry, you usually get an appetite when you go to your favorite restaurant. Whether or not you have academic or personal worries, you tend to forget them when you go to the baseball stadium to watch your favorite team play. Whether or not you are sleepy, you generally fall asleep if you brush your teeth and crawl into bed.

In each example, the environment is very closely connected by habit to specific activities and emotions. Psychologists have discovered that this connection or habit becomes stronger each time you go to that place. If you understand this principle, you can use it to help create an environment in which you can work.

You should have two places where you work and do nothing else: the library and a desk at home. Whenever you go to either of these places, you should work. Never read magazines, novels, or socialize (e.g., talk on the telephone from your desk) in these places. Similarly, do not try to study on your bed or while watching TV. The bed and TV are associated with activities (sleeping and entertainment) that will compete with studying. Being able to study, once you decide to, often requires willpower and concentration. It's important to shut out competing thoughts and distractions. If you have places associated with work and not with play, it will become easier and easier to get started and to concentrate whenever you go to those places.

When (Managing Your Time)

Develop a rough schedule of when you intend to work. Assuming that your schoolwork is a top-priority item (otherwise you would probably be working full time at a job), try to schedule this work for the hours *when you are at your best*. Some people are sharpest and most efficient first thing in the morning, some people don't get going until the afternoon, and others concentrate best in the evening. Classes you expect to be particularly difficult or that require you to participate frequently (e.g., seminars) or that have many quizzes should be scheduled during this time. Otherwise, try to schedule your classes (and your part-time job) for your less efficient time in order to keep the good time free for studying. Studying usually requires more effort from you than attending class and taking notes. You have to get started by yourself, keep your mind on the task, think creatively, come up with questions, and organize information.

Here is an example of the hours you might budget for class, studying, personal responsibilities, and social and recreational activities. A rule of thumb is that you should expect to spend at least three hours studying for every hour in class.

Sample Schedule

On the following page is a schedule for a student who is taking four courses, requiring 12 hours per week in class (shown with an "X"). As you can see, the student has planned on being in the library to work or look up information between classes or at times when the dorm is usually noisy (Friday afternoon). Total study time is about 38 hours (14 in library, 24 at home). Friday and Saturday are set aside for social and other recreational activities. Thursday night and Sunday morning are personal. There are still a few additional hours that could be used for studying, relaxing, or whatever.

Exactly What (Managing What You Do)

You are at your desk during budgeted study time. What should you do? This is often surprisingly hard to decide unless you have made a plan in advance. Get a large calendar at the beginning of each semester and, looking at all your course outlines, fill in the weekly assignments, exam dates (as best you know them), and due dates for term papers, lab reports, etc. If the first exam for a course is in four weeks and covers eight chapters, spread out the reading over the four weeks. Write down how many chapters you want to cover each week. When you schedule your reading, remember that textbooks are usually written with chapters of about equal length, but often the easier material comes first; you need to allow for the reading to become more difficult as you progress through the book. Also, you have to allow time to review your text and lecture notes during the last week before the exam (see Chapter 5).

Term papers and research reports present a special problem, because you must break them down into smaller parts yourself and decide how much time to allow for each; for example, two weeks for library research,

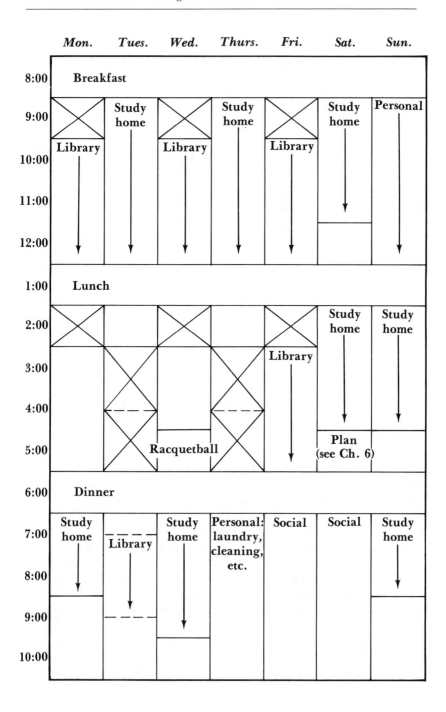

one week for developing an outline of the paper, two weeks for the first draft, one week for further library research, one week for revising, and one week for final typing. Usually you will not have any one week to spend entirely on any one course or project. An overall schedule worked out at the beginning of the semester will let you see whether your work plan is reasonable, before you misjudge your time so much that you are in a mess. Also, if you can't keep up with this plan in the first few weeks, it will be clear to you before the add-drop deadline (see Chapter 2) that you are in over your head.

In addition to a term plan, you will need more specific plans for each week and day. Set a time to develop a detailed plan for each week. Friday afternoon of the week before is usually a good time, because people often have a Friday afternoon slump when it may be hard to concentrate on other tasks. Sunday night or the first thing Monday morning are also possibilities. It's important to plan at the same time each week, so it becomes a habit. Weekly planning allows you to make changes in the term plan to take into account new assignments, unexpected problems with the material in a particular course, being ahead of schedule in some classes, etc.

CHOOSE ONE:
A) "I'LL JUST LIE DOWN FOR A LITTLE WHILE."
B) "I'LL GET UP EARLY AND FINISH IT."
C) "I CAN'T CONCENTRATE VERY WELL RIGHT NOW ANYWAY."

While the term plan helps you spread the work out over the entire semester or quarter, it is still quite general. The weekly plan should specify *exactly what* you are going to accomplish *when* and *where* for each day of the week. Those things that are hardest, most important, or contribute most to your grade should be scheduled for your hours of peak concentration and efficiency. When you define tasks, be specific. You can't accomplish a vague idea such as "know the material in Chapter 10." What does "know" mean (see Chapter 4)?

You have to write down something you can actually achieve such as "make an outline of Chapter 10" or "be able to define and give an example of each of the seven most important concepts in Chapter 10." One reason studying is stressful for many students is that they never know when they have done enough or when they should move on to the next task. If your goal has been specific enough, you'll have the satisfaction of being able to reach it. The more success you have in reaching these goals, the more pleasant studying will be.

Here is a sample plan for a student whose best period is in the morning.

Weekly Plan for a Morning Person

This student is taking four courses: Biology, Art History, English, and Statistics.

Main Goal for Week: Get Started on Art Term Paper!

Monday

Library	10–11 a.m.	Art: List three possible term paper topics
	11–1 p.m.	Statistics: Chapter 4, first three problems
Home	7–9 p.m.	Biology: Outline Chapter 3

Tuesday

Home	9–11 a.m.	Statistics: Last four problems due Thursday
	11–1 p.m.	English: Read 80 pages of *Great Expectations*
Library	7:30–9:30 p.m.	Art: Check card catalog for available material on term paper topics

Wednesday

Library	10–12 a.m.	Biology: Outline Chapter 4
	12–1 p.m.	Art: Look up references, browse through stacks
Home	7–8 p.m.	Biology: Review notes from Chapters 3 and 4, lectures
	8–10 p.m.	English: Read 80 pages of *Great Expectations*

Thursday

Home	9–11 a.m.	Statistics: Read Chapter 5
	11–1 p.m.	Art: Decide on term paper topic

Friday

Library	10–12 a.m.	Art: References
	12–1 p.m.	Art: Write three questions term paper might answer
	3–5 p.m.	Finish unfinished work from this week

As you can see, this plan has several features. Tasks are defined very specifically. The more challenging tasks (for this person) are scheduled for the morning. Time is budgeted for using the library. The plan notes the due-dates for assignments, and time is allowed for finishing tasks that could not be completed earlier in the week in the time allotted. If you write in your schedule each week what you actually spend this makeup time on, it will soon be clear if you are underestimating the time a particular course will take.

Go over the plan for the day the first thing *every* morning. You won't have to spend much time deciding what to do or where to go—simply follow the plan for the day. When you don't follow it, it's a good idea to write down what you have done instead. Later you will know where your time went, and you may learn something about how to schedule your time in the future. For example, you may be leaving out some necessary activities such as allowing time for friends.

Managing Your Mind

Ah, but is it so simple as all that? No, it isn't *that* simple. If it were, we would all accomplish a lot more than we do. But you can learn to get better and better at managing your time, allowing you to accomplish more and have more time for fun as well. Learning to manage your time should be a major goal in itself. You may often fail to live up to a plan, but if you look at the things that make you fail, you will learn something valuable about yourself, the distractions in your life, and your real priorities. You can then use this information to help make a better schedule and to help you stick to it in the future.

Procrastination

One of the most dangerous threats to reaching goals is procrastination. You can procrastinate in many ways; the most obvious is going to the movies instead of working out those chemistry equations. A subtler form of procrastination, however, is when you don't carefully consider the real importance of various tasks.

For example, you could spend a whole day working on a challenging extra credit "mind-teaser" problem given by your calculus professor, instead of getting started on that history term paper. You would have been better off to have spent two hours on the mind-teaser *after* you had spent at least two hours working on the term paper. Or, you might decide to work on the term paper after you have finished all of your reading for the week. But some of that reading is less important and would be easier to rush through if you become pressed for time. Some tasks simply cannot be rushed such as working out statistics problems or getting reference material from the library.

Priorities

Another dangerous threat to reaching goals is failure to consider your priorities. You must decide the relative value of each task and try to set your priorities accordingly. By setting priorities you face two facts: (1) you aren't going to be able to do everything on any particular day or in any particular week (or in any particular lifetime!); and (2) some things are more important to you than others. If you can't do everything, it's clear that you should always work on the most important thing first, then the next most important thing, and so on *in order.* Setting priorities also helps you budget time in relation to the value of something. If 80% of the questions on the exam will come from the text and lectures, you can't afford to spend 75% of your study time on the supplementary readings.

What is most important may change from day to day or week to week depending on how you are doing in your courses, what due dates are coming up, what new assignments have been made, etc. That's why you should spend a few minutes each morning reviewing your weekly plan and making any necessary adjustments in the priorities and schedule for the day. Then, follow the plan, doing one thing at a time.

Many students say they have trouble concentrating. There could be many reasons for this—they have a noisy workplace, they aren't getting enough sleep, they aren't eating well. However, one of the most likely reasons is that they have not defined tasks clearly enough for themselves, so they aren't sure exactly what they should be concentrating on. Or, they

may not be doing the most important thing on their list. If you are working on the least important thing on your list before the most important, chances are you will find it hard to concentrate, because in the back of your mind you will be worrying about that more important task.

If you do the more important things first, you will probably do the less important projects more efficiently and with more enjoyment when you get to them. Also, if you know you have planned some time in your schedule for a task, it is easier to put it out of your mind in the meantime.

Try to recognize when you are avoiding a difficult or important task by keeping busy at something that is less so. This is not a problem you can solve in one term. You will be faced with it over and over throughout your life, both in your career and in your personal life.

Sticking to It

People who get a lot done, who seem to accomplish a lot in their work and still have time for vacations, hobbies, and friends, have learned to control their time by learning to manage their state of mind. For example, efficient people have tricks to control their level of motivation. To make themselves get started or stick to something, they set up games and rewards. For example, find a friend of about your same ability to compete with. Whoever finishes the calculus problems last pays for the after-study beer. Compete with yourself. Try to read more today than you did yesterday. Keep score. Every time you read and outline 25 pages of that economics text, give yourself 10 points. When you have 100 points, buy those new jogging shorts that you don't really need. Check your progress. If you have allowed an hour to skim a book, set a timer for 20 minutes to see if you are a third of the way through.

In summary, the way to manage your time is to use a number of techniques. Make decisions in advance about what to do each week and eliminate the constant indecision about what to do next that takes up so much time. Manage your environment so that you will have a place where you expect to work and where there are no distractions from TV, friends, children, etc. Realize that big tasks that seem impossible are made up of a lot of little tasks that are possible, so make yourself break that big job into separate smaller ones. Concentrate on one part at a time and forget your fear of the whole. Keep in mind your priorities and ask yourself often if you are doing the most important thing on your list or if you have gotten sidetracked onto less important activities.

If you are having a very difficult time doing something, break it down into even smaller parts and tell yourself that you have to do at least one of them. If you have found the assigned journal article in the library, it isn't so hard to read the introduction to see what it's about. If that's all you get done, fine. Something is better than nothing, and you can try another small part tomorrow. But by at least starting (reading one page or doing one problem or writing one paragraph), you give yourself the chance to keep going and eventually to finish. Once you've read the introduction, you might not find it so difficult to keep reading, and so on. Success brings more success. When you have completed one small part, it no longer seems so hard to try the next one. The box for "Rules for Managing Your Time" summarizes our advice.

Rules for Managing Your Time

- Set aside times and places for work
- Set priorities and then *do* things in priority order
- Break large tasks into much smaller ones
- Keep the tasks planned for a day down to a reasonable number
- Work on one thing at a time (an important task)
- Define all tasks specifically (in terms of what you want to have written or want to be able to recall, etc.)
- Check your progress often
- Compete with yourself or a friend
- Reward yourself (enjoy your successes!)

Do More Than Study

For Your Mind

While colleges vary in how many different plays, concerts, art exhibits, movies, and lectures are going on at any one time, even the smallest college is usually rich in these opportunities. They are often free to students or at prices much below similar events in the nearby towns or cities. They are usually listed in an "Events Section" of the school newspaper or advertised on bulletin boards. Check these out each week.

If you don't know what a string quartet sounds like, go find out. Do you like jazz? Try it. Sit in on the public lecture on problems in restoring great art works. Go see what the photographs taken by your fellow students look like. Spend a few minutes at lunch browsing through an exhibit of African or Indian artifacts in the anthropology museum. Make attending some (e.g., two per month) of these events a regular, planned part of your schedule. They are part of your education. If you are bored at college, you probably haven't stopped to think about what a gold mine you are sitting on.

For Your Body

Colleges also usually give you the chance to learn and play a wide range of sports — swimming, tennis, fencing, horseback riding, track, racquetball, gymnastics, basketball, baseball, volleyball, etc. You don't have to be a "star" athlete to be active, belong to a team, or just have fun with a friend.

There are several ways to get involved in sports. Taking a course is probably the easiest way to learn something new (in fact at some colleges it is required), or you can just set aside some fixed time in your schedule to get together with one or more friends for a game or two. You may have to reserve or schedule a court or your gym space ahead of time so look into how you do this. Usually the space is free or available for a very small charge to students. (The same facilities in private clubs would cost you quite a bit, so take advantage while you can.)

Finally, colleges often have organized *intramural* leagues where, for example, teams from different departments, dorms, clubs, and so forth play against each other. You don't "try out" for intramural teams, you just join. This is an excellent way to give yourself the motivation and structure to play regularly, and you'll improve your skills and your health and meet people at the same time.

7.

The Grade Gremlin

HOW DO PROFESSORS DECIDE GRADES?

If you were to take a poll of college students to find out what they liked least about college, you would probably find grades high up on the list, maybe right at the top. If you were to ask professors that question, you would probably get the same answer. What is going on here? Why *use* grades if nobody seems to like them?

In this chapter we'll try to answer this question and tell you something about how professors determine grades. We'll also discuss what to do if you get a grade you feel you don't deserve. While we don't think this chapter will turn you into someone who enjoys being graded, we believe taking the mystery out of grades will help you deal with them.

Why Bother Grading at All?

Grades are a form of evaluation. Your performance on a test, a paper, or in an entire course is compared to a set of standards. At most colleges, an "A" is given for outstanding work, and a "B" means better than adequate performance. The famous "gentleman's C" has traditionally been for adequate work, while "D" is barely passing, and "F" is failing. To compute your **grade point average** (the average of all your grades or G.P.A.), these letters are usually assigned a point value — A = 4, B = 3, C = 2, D = 1, F = 0. The points corresponding to each of your letter grades are multiplied by the number of credits or units for the corresponding course, then added up and divided by the number of credits or units you took.

Employers and graduate schools use grades to help them decide which applicants they want. More importantly, grades can be valuable to you because they tell you how you are doing. You can use this information to choose other courses and possibly to select a career. It's usually a mistake to spend your life trying to succeed at something you aren't good at.

A major problem is that a grade is a single letter or number, even though many different things affect it, for example, time spent studying, talent, how you were feeling the day of the final, where you go to school, and just plain luck (or lack of it). How, then, can anyone argue that grades should be used for any of the major decisions we just mentioned? The most honest answer is that grades are not perfect, but they are the best things we have. Used along with other types of information, grades do seem to do their job.

In the late 1960s and early 1970s, some colleges and universities moved away from traditional grading. Students could take many of their courses on a Pass/No Credit basis, and some colleges used written evaluations in place of letter grades. In addition, at some colleges the meaning of particular letter grades was unofficially changed; a "B," rather than a "C," came to mean average work.

Now ten years later, as the 1980s begin, we find most colleges shifting back to the old system. One reason for the change is that graduate schools and employers complained that Pass/No Credit grades didn't give them any way to choose among applicants. They were then forced to use only standardized tests and letters of recommendation from faculty to make their decisions. Letters of recommendation can be very useful, but few students get to know several professors well. Standardized tests are useful, too, but depend on a student's performance on just one day.

Surprisingly, many students *also* wanted to go back to the old system. Many began to worry that a system *without* grades was more unfair than one *with* grades. Even under systems without grades, professors are asked to make evaluations and recommendations about students. They can't help but be influenced by personality, appearance, and whether people share their points of view or values. Without information based on tests and papers, these other things tend to become more important in influencing a professor's opinion. In addition, many students noticed that they didn't work as hard without grades as they had with them.

There has been a move back then to traditional grading at colleges and universities throughout the country. Ten years of change, however, have had an important effect. Faculty, graduate schools, and employers are now more aware of the limits of grades.

How Do Professors Determine Grades?

Several different ways are possible. One is the *absolute standard* method. In most cases, your professor has a pretty clear idea of what s/he wants you to take away from a course and how it can be measured. The professor can set rough guidelines for what would be adequate college-level performance, more than adequate, etc. These guidelines, set in advance of seeing how the class did, are then used to assign grades. With this approach, everyone in the class would get A's if each student met the professor's standards for outstanding performance. On the other hand, everyone might get a C if each person's work was about what the professor felt was adequate.

At the other extreme, some professors take an entirely *relative* (as opposed to absolute) approach to grading. This relative method is based on the fact that most human abilities and characteristics vary in the same way as heights and weights. A few people are very tall, and a few are very short, but most fall in the middle. Things that look like this follow what is called the normal curve. Some professors, particularly those with very large classes, assume that performance in their courses will look like this too. This approach is also known as "grading on the curve." With this system there are always some people getting A's, some getting F's, and most getting C's.

Most professors use a grading system that falls somewhere in the middle of the two we have just described. They have a good idea of what outstanding or adequate performance in their course would be, but they also want their grades to take into account the kind of students they are teaching.

Professors also differ in how they put several grades together to make a final course grade. Some drop your lowest exam score, some count certain exams more heavily than others, and some use other measures along with exam scores to determine the grade. Most will tell you how they do it on the first day of class. Write it down so you will have the information later when it will mean more to you. If a professor forgets to discuss grading, it is alright to ask how the final grades will be figured out.

A Bad Grade

Receiving a D or an F usually hurts, but being depressed about it doesn't help. Look at the grade as information. It could mean you're not spending enough time on your course work, or that you don't have the necessary study skills. Both of these situations can be corrected (see Chapters 4, 5, and 6). A bad grade may mean you don't have any particular talent for something, and this is also important to know. There may be times in your life when you've done the best you can, and maybe it's not very good, but it's unrealistic to expect to be terrific at everything. Graduate schools, professional schools, and employers look at your whole college record, not just the one bad grade you're depressed about. On the other hand, if you have many bad grades spread over several different terms, it is an important signal to you. This is not very likely to be due simply to "bad breaks."

What Can You Learn From a Bad Grade?

If you get a bad grade on a test, you can usually use it to tell you which of your study skills (Chapters 4 and 5) needs work—and this will tell you how to improve your grade the next time. Look at the test carefully. Almost always you got something right—some multiple-choice questions or nearly full credit on one or more essays. Even though it may feel like a total disaster at first, even a test you got an F on is usually not entirely a disaster at all. Use the difference between the good and bad parts to guide you.

Are all the essays bad and all the multiple-choice questions correct? Then you need to practice writing essays. You might even ask the professor if you can try rewriting the essays to see if you can do it right. Ask if your instructor will regrade them—not for more credit, but because you want to learn. You can look at your friends' good essays for guidance if our suggestions aren't enough. When students ask for this kind of help, professors are very impressed and follow the student's progress with interest—much more than is given to the usual F student.

What if you got some multiple-choice and some essays wrong? If you look at the questions, surprisingly often you will discover that most of your mistakes are *either* in questions based on the reading *or* in those based on lectures. That is, you are not bad at everything. Obviously, if you see this kind of pattern, work on your weak points—taking lecture notes or reading notes. Use our hints and if possible compare your own reading and lecture notes with those of an "A" student friend.

A different problem you may see when you look over your exam is that there were one or two whole topics you didn't understand at all. You got almost every question on cell division wrong, for example. If you think back, you will probably find that you knew you were weak in that area. You avoided studying it. It made you nervous to think about it. Next time you feel that way about something, take the feeling seriously as a warning. Work extra hard on that area. If necessary, you can ask the professor for help. If you can narrow down the problem, s/he will usually be glad to help.

What if You Think You've Been Treated Unfairly?

Students sometimes get a bad grade when they feel they deserve a better one. Most faculty try hard to be fair and at the same time to set standards at the right level for a college. But grading often involves judgment and opinion, and you may feel you have a good argument for a higher grade. Professors also make mistakes, and it is not hard to miss something after reading 200 essay exams!

How to Appeal an Exam Grade

If you believe you deserve more credit on an exam than you were given, make an appointment to talk it over with the person who graded your paper. Except for arithmetic errors (such as the wrong point total), it is best to save discussion of grades until you can sit down with the professor during office hours. *Avoid* the temptation to rush up to a professor at the end of a class when exams are handed back.

Most professors dislike the time right after exams are returned because grades, and not learning, seem to be the only thing some students care about. Keeping in mind how the professor is probably feeling can help you when you go to see him or her. Be specific about why you think your answer is more complete than the grade suggests. Try to let the professor know you want to understand *why* your answer was not good enough so you can do better next time. Don't quibble over a few points, and don't try to pressure a professor with irrelevant remarks about your plans for medical school, your draft status, the position you play on the basketball team, etc. Like most people, professors get angry when they feel they are being unfairly pressured, and an angry professor may not be as interested in your grade.

One important thing to remember while taking exams and when going over them after they are graded is that your professor must grade what you wrote—not what you meant to write or what you really knew but had buried deep within your subconscious. This is probably the single most common problem students have when taking exams. If this seems to happen to you again and again, talk it over with your professor to see what you can do about it. Otherwise, the problem is not likely to go away.

Appealing a Final Grade

Up to this point we have been talking about how to appeal a grade on an exam or paper. It may be, however, that you feel your final grade is not fair. The best approach is to talk to your professor, going prepared with a folder containing all of your exams and papers for the course. Ask how the final grades were determined. If you still feel you have a case, ask the professor to look over your work in the course *at his or her leisure*. (When pushed to make a fast decision, they are likely to say "no.") Make an appointment to come back to discuss the final decision and to pick up your papers. Be courteous and pleasant: little is ever gained (and much can be lost) by rude behavior.

If you are still not satisfied and feel you have a strong case, most colleges have a formal procedure for appealing grades. Most disagreements about grades, though, amount to disagreements about standards. The people who make the final decision usually feel that setting standards is the professor's, not the student's, job. There are some cases where an appeal can help you, however, and you should know that it is possible. If the procedure for appealing a grade is not in the college catalog, ask someone in the undergraduate advising office how to go about it.

If You Decide Not to Appeal

Suppose you don't agree with your professor's decision, but at the same time you don't feel your case is appropriate to appeal. How should you deal with this? You'll have to accept it. Sometimes unfair things happen, and it is understandable if you are unhappy or angry about it for a while. It would be a big mistake, though, to let that unhappiness spread beyond the situation that started it. Becoming bitter about "the system" or hostile toward professors in general will work to your disadvantage. You wouldn't want a professor to punish you because some other student cheated or failed to show for an appointment or had 12 different excuses for not getting a paper in on time. You wouldn't want the professor to become cynical about students in general because of these bad experiences and to stop treating students as individuals. It's only fair that you try to keep your bad experiences in perspective as well.

Incompletes

A professor gives each student a grade at the end of the term showing that s/he has judged the quality of the student's work. A special grade at many colleges is the **I** or **incomplete.** This is typically used when for reasons the student can't control s/he can't finish the work in a course on time. Reasons for incompletes include severe health problems or a death in the family. Some colleges and some faculty members will give an incomplete to any student who wants one, but generally this grade is used only in very special circumstances.

Whether or not your college or professor is willing to give incompletes, you should avoid them whenever possible. Suppose you are at the end of the term with only a week to finish a term paper, and you feel you could use another three weeks; you may be tempted to ask a professor for an incomplete. Most students who get incompletes for this kind of reason promise themselves they will do a terrific job on the paper over intersession or during the summer. Typically, though, they don't. If you are like most students, the paper will hang over your head during this time, producing many guilty moments, but you won't actually begin working on it until you are nearing the deadline. You may spend a week or two finishing the paper, but the extra time will be largely used up on "getting back into it." In the end, the paper probably will be no better, and may be even a little worse, than what you would have written with a big push at the end of the semester.

For the same reasons, it is a bad idea to postpone a test just because you don't feel "ready" to take it. Finally, if you're trying to finish the work for incompletes from last term during the current semester, the old courses will act like an **overload** (see pages 116–117) and may give you a bad start in your new classes.

If, on the other hand, some serious situation develops in your life where an incomplete seems to be the best solution, talk it over with your professor. However, incompletes are rarely a solution to the problem of just failing to "get your act together." Even if faculty are willing to give them, it's not necessarily a favor.

8.

Creative Coping

Many things will compete with your studies for your time, energy, intelligence, and creativity. Some of these things are fun, and some are awful, but all will distract you. Most students will face at least one of the situations we will describe in this chapter at some time during their college career. The rest of your life won't stop while you're going to college. Look around you. Many of the people who are doing well in their classes are dealing successfully with these other important areas of their life.

Coping With Others

College is likely to be a time when relationships with other people are especially complicated or intense.

Parents

Whether or not you live with your parents, you may feel like you can't get away from them. Their beliefs and expectations may seem to be part of your daily life, something you are conscious of all the time. You may have trouble getting along with them, or you may have a problem gaining your independence. A few lucky people just fall into a comfortable adult relationship with their parents. For most of us, however, it takes work and sometimes a lot of misunderstanding and pain.

Your adult relationship with your parents should be different from the one you had with them as a child. This will probably take some effort from you to bring about. One thing that may help you keep calm is to remember that your parents have been taking care of you or worrying about you for years, and it's very hard for them to stop. If you think about how they feel, you may come up with little things to do that aren't much trouble for you but will make this change easier for them (and, therefore, for you!).

One problem for many students is that their parents seem to be clinging to them — always calling and writing. These same students will never write or call, because they hear so much from their family as it is. Think of it from the parents' side: it's as if their child went to college and dropped into a black hole. They don't know if you are too depressed to write, too overworked to write, having too much fun to write, or were mugged the first day of classes and have been in a coma ever since. If you are away from home for the first time, you should write at least a short note or card every two weeks. This will do wonders to ease their anxiety about you.

Some parents will be satisfied to know their child is okay, happy they don't have to worry any more, and eager to get on with their own lives. For other parents, their child is the center of their lives. If your parents fall into this second group, your problem will be to grow and move out of the center of their lives, hurting them as little as possible. Regular letters help here, too. Also, if you live close enough to see your parents occasionally, don't always let them be the ones to suggest a visit. If you ask to see them sometimes, they will feel you *want* to see them. Then, when you have to, it is easier for you to say "no" without hurting their feelings.

Another common problem comes up when you try to tell your parents that your thinking has changed on many things, because of what you have learned at college. Don't bombard them all at once with all your new ideas and moral values. Also, you can't tell them about some new idea or lifestyle you're thinking about and then expect them *not* to tell you what they think about it.

If you feel your parents are pressing in on you, you may be asking for it without realizing it. Are you giving them mixed messages? You can't lean on your parents for money and for support in all the practical details of daily living, and then expect them not to express any opinions about what you do. If you need your parents to know about and approve of everything you do is this because you genuinely want to share every part of your life with them? Or is it because you have fallen into the habit of baiting them, enjoying the chance to tell them things you know will upset them?

Family

Some students live in family situations where they have a lot of responsibilities. They may have a wife or husband, children, or younger brothers and sisters they help care for. These students may hear complaints such as "We never do anything together anymore." They may feel guilty about going to school, because they help less around the house or bring in less money. If they've been out of school for a while, they may have special problems (see Chapter 11) and feel like they don't have any spare time to be interested in what others are doing.

Every once in a while, talk with your family about what you feel you are getting out of college. It helps for people to remind each other occasionally about why they are making sacrifices. When the sacrifices are greater than any of you expected, try to talk it out calmly. More importantly, give yourself and the people around you a break. Take a morning, afternoon, or entire day off every once in a while and help with a family project or just have fun. When you take time off, *forget* about school. Don't spend the whole time worrying about what you have to do. It's no fun for anyone if you are constantly talking about how far behind you are.

Friends

There may be times when you yourself don't have any problems, but when you have at least one friend undergoing a major crisis. If you have some common sense and a sympathetic ear, you may become the "dorm therapist." Talking a problem over with a friend can be very helpful, and sharing problems and solutions brings people closer together. You also learn a lot. Whether it is your problem or the other person's, you get ideas for the future about how to deal with things that can happen to anyone.

Ideally, these sorts of relationships go two ways—you get as much support as you give. However, if you find yourself becoming the Rock of Gibraltar for the entire household or dorm, you are making a mistake. Constantly dealing with crises can tire you out and leave you with less energy for the rest of your life, including your studies. Perhaps more importantly, you can become tempted to handle situations that are, in fact, beyond you. For example, a friend who is pregnant needs not only the interest of friends but specific and accurate counseling and medical treatment as soon as possible. Friends who are depressed to the point of thinking about suicide or who have become dependent on alcohol or other drugs need professional help.

In these situations, *it is not fair to the friend* to try to handle it yourself. You may be keeping him or her from solutions you would never have thought of. If such severe situations come up, one way you can be extremely helpful is to offer to go with or to take your friend to a doctor, clinic, or hospital. Even for everyday problems, going to a doctor is frightening for many people, especially if they feel they may have to make important decisions alone right on-the-spot. You can be there to give emotional support and to remind them that asking for information does not necessarily mean they have to agree to a particular treatment.

Romance

You may be seeing someone regularly and enjoying it or not seeing someone regularly and not enjoying it. On the other hand, you may be seeing someone regularly and *not* enjoying it or not seeing anyone in particular and enjoying it. This is a topic whose possibilities are so vast we hesitate to say anything about it at all! Few things are as interesting as a romance when it is going well or take as much energy when it is going badly. However it is going, though, romance (or no romance) can certainly compete with studies for your attention. So, we will offer a few observations.

A college campus provides many opportunities to meet people (see the section on loneliness later in this chapter). If you are shy, college is a great place to practice social skills. So many people are coping with the same problems, they are willing to overlook other people's mistakes. Also, many activities take place in groups, so no one person has to do everything to "keep things going." In any event, you are likely to get a second chance soon, either with the same person or with another.

The better you get to know the campus, the easier it will be to spot chances to get acquainted, so don't worry if nothing happens right away. If you want to meet people of a certain type (Methodists, backpackers, socialists), there are many ways (the clubs you join, the courses you take, the meetings you go to) to increase your chances of getting to know people with values or interests like yours. If your interests are really offbeat, you can always start a new group yourself!

In our culture these days, people differ in what they expect from a relationship: romance but not sex, sex but not romance, both but no commitments, both with commitments, etc. If you have fairly firm ideas about what you want, you will probably be better off looking for someone with ideas similar to yours than you will be trying to persuade someone with extremely different ideas to see it your way. Why stay involved in a constant battle?

All adults should know the basics about how their bodies work and how to stay healthy (see Chapter 12). If your idea of a relationship includes sex, you owe it to yourself and your partner to know in advance about venereal disease, the biology of reproduction, and contraception. Don't be embarrassed about what you suspect you don't know. More importantly, don't, like so many people, *overestimate* what you already know. Mistaken ideas about these topics are very common and produce a shockingly large number of unwanted pregnancies on college campuses. There is also currently an epidemic of venereal diseases among college students. Untreated venereal disease can lead to serious complications.

It is easy for college students to get accurate information about almost any topic. There is always the library or nearby bookstore (some readable possibilities are given at the end of Chapter 12). Certain biology and psychology courses cover sex and reproduction. The health center, local clinics, and groups such as Planned Parenthood provide free advice, literature, and references. You may feel it is unromantic to plan your love life. Believe us, there is nothing romantic about abortion, adoption, or unwanted babies—and that's where unplanned sexual activity leads with amazing efficiency. If you can't plan, either abstain or be prepared for the consequences. Taking charge of your life always pays off, but here the payoff is particularly obvious.

Peer Pressure

Many students are between the ages of 17 and 23, a time when it is particularly painful to feel that people of your own age do not think well of you. You may know how you want to spend your time and what you want to believe, but the people around you may be sending another message: "Enough studying, let's have a party" or "The demonstration is more important than math problems" or "How can you miss this great concert to write your paper?"

You may have decided it is important to keep your grades as high as possible to give yourself future choices. The friends you spend your time with may have different values and seem to be criticizing yours. Or, what if you're involved in a romantic relationship and doing better academically than the other person? Does this make him or her uncomfortable and does s/he say things, such as "Grades aren't important" or "Education courses are all easy," that discourage you?

The truth is, much of the time we can disagree with or say "no" to our friends without losing their interest, respect, or loyalty. They may kid you a little if you act differently from the group, but most groups can stand (and even appreciate) some individuality from their members. Most of us are probably more afraid than we need be about what others will think if we don't agree with them about something or don't do what they'd like us to. If you are finding it hard to keep from going along with things you would rather not do, you are probably overestimating what being yourself will cost you.

If you *are* in a group or relationship in which you have to make compromises that aren't good for you, there is probably nothing else to do but find other relationships. This may seem scary, but remember that you got your current friends (e.g., roommates) partly by chance. Can you do worse in finding new friends, now that you know more about what you are looking for?

Social and Political Activities

Part of the excitement of college is seeing the relationship between ideas in books and events actually going on now. There is no limit to the number of issues to become involved in: migrant workers, nuclear energy, gay rights, state politics, foreign policy, women's rights, volunteer tutoring of children with learning disabilities, etc. Being part of these events will add new dimensions to your life. There is a danger, though, that their importance may sometimes seem so great or exciting that you ignore course work. If this happens more than occasionally, you can expect your grades to suffer. This may not be a problem for you if you don't have any career goals requiring more than passing grades. If, on the other hand, you find yourself most likely to be swept up in important issues right around midterms or finals, you should think about whether you are using your activities to avoid studying.

Coping With Yourself

Everyone can sometimes be in a bad mood, but maybe you feel anxious or depressed all the time. There are a number of common reasons for these feelings.

Feeling Helpless or Overwhelmed by School Work

We have spent a good part of this book describing skills you need to cope with course work. Many students only need a few tips about how to study or how to talk to a faculty member to feel as if they have some control over their lives. However, you may need more than the tips in this book. If you feel there isn't anything you can do to help yourself, try talking about your situation with either a private therapist or someone from the campus psychological clinic if there is one available. It also might be a good time to think about "stopping out" (see page 120).

Questioning Religious Beliefs

College is a time when you might begin to question long-held beliefs, especially about religion. You may come to doubt your faith, or you may for the first time find some religious faith. Whether you are losing a faith or gaining one, you may find it useful to talk about your feelings with a member of the clergy who is not directly connected with the decision you are making. Many campuses have chaplains or clergy from different faiths. These people often talk to students in your situation and can be a sounding board for your thoughts or give you ideas you may have missed. While not all of these people will necessarily have anything to say to you that will be of use, chances are you will at least understand your own thoughts better if you try putting them into words.

You might enjoy taking some theology or history of religion courses. A major point to remember is that decisions about values, religions, or philosophies are generally not made in a day. Whatever you do, don't let yourself be pressured by others, whether it is to leave a religion or to join one. If the issue is complicated and important, why shouldn't it take you a while to think about it?

Loneliness

This is so common, and yet with all the people on a college campus how could anybody be lonely? People are lonely partly because they are afraid

THERE'S GOT TO BE MORE TO LIFE THAN A NEAT ROOM.

to talk to people they don't know, so they don't get to know anybody. A college campus is one of the easiest places to meet someone, because there is almost always a topic of interest to both of you. It's perfectly okay to strike up a conversation with a person waiting outside a classroom or with someone sitting next to you in class before it begins. Invite somebody for coffee after class or as a study break.

Both men and women should learn to start conversations with people of both sexes. Don't think of every social situation as a "date." Make friends with people who have similar interests. Even if you are slow to meet new people, don't just hang around with your old high school crowd; it's hard to be a new you with people who already know the old you. There are many clubs and interest groups on almost every college campus. Join a few: the school newspaper, a political group, the volleyball team, or the German Club. If you don't find a club that interests you, start one that does.

Crush on a Professor or Graduate Student

It's not unusual for students to develop crushes on teachers. Some instructors are dynamic lecturers, others are generous about helping you. Some are incredibly smart. Others seem cute or vulnerable or just like very nice people. Sometimes, too, people in positions of power or authority seem attractive, even if they aren't very nice. Whether or not the crush is on a professor of the same or opposite sex, these crushes generally do not lead to a real romance (see Chapter 3). Don't worry about it, don't dwell on it, don't spend time in fantasies involving a closer relationship with the person—but do enjoy the crush. It can make a class more interesting, and it can make you want to do a better job academically. If you admire or respect or care about someone, you are more likely to want to please him or her. The appropriate way to express these feelings is by doing the best possible work you can in the course.

Drugs and Alcohol

Alcohol and other drugs (from caffeine to heroin) are easily available on or near most college campuses. Many students have already experimented with these drugs in high school, some will take them for the first time at college, and some will pass up such "opportunities" altogether. You will develop your own views about the value of drinking and taking drugs and about the part you want these activities to play in your life.

Whenever you are using drugs or thinking about it (including those prescribed by doctors such as valium or other tranquilizers), you should try to evaluate their health risk. Our best guess is that scientists and medical researchers will continue to discover undesirable side effects from even moderate, regular use of almost all drugs, including those many of us take without thinking about it at all, for example, caffeine. Not long ago, no one worried about nicotine, caffeine, aspirin, or the moderate use of alcohol. Now doctors know these drugs can also cause problems in certain situations.

There is no question that *heavy* use of alcohol and many other drugs, such as marijuana, cocaine, heroin, amphetamines, barbiturates, angel dust, etc., can be disastrous for your personal and academic life at college. To yourself, you may seem happier and more interesting, exciting, witty, or glamorous with the help of drugs, but to someone else, you may only seem more aggravating, childish, or boring. Students who become especially dependent on drugs usually become a burden for friends, and this can only put a strain on relationships. Studying or going to class stoned will typically reduce the amount of material you learn.

"Heavy use," of course, depends on the drug, but you should be concerned if you even suspect you are falling into a pattern of heavy drug use. Some signs are: Do you almost always get drunk when you drink? Do you have to have something to drink more than once a week? Is it hard for you to "concentrate" without taking something? Do you often feel you can't read or work on a paper without having a joint? These are signals that you should get help in finding other ways of coping with social or academic problems. Check with your campus health service (see Chapter 12) or psychological clinic to see what is available.

Financial Worries

Worrying about money can use up a lot of energy. There are many tricks to budgeting your money to make it go as far as possible. You can save a lot of money if you can get by with a bike instead of a car, for example. Or a group of people can buy groceries together to take advantage of quantity discounts.

Many students carry a full academic load and work up to ten hours a week. If you have to work more than ten hours a week to make ends meet, be *sure* to reduce your course load. Students who try to carry a full load and work half-time, or more, often find themselves run ragged by the middle of the term. Many campuses have a financial aid office where students can find out about scholarships and loan programs. Part-time jobs on campus are often handled by a job placement office. Talk to other students and find out how they manage. Some people have had more experience than others making up a budget and sticking to it, and students can learn from each other about how to handle this problem.

Tragedies

You may suddenly be faced with a family situation, such as the death of a close relative, that requires you to be away from your classwork for several days. If you will miss taking an exam or turning in an assignment, you should let your instructors know the situation. Similarly, if a severe or long-lasting problem with your own health develops, let your instructors know so that they can help you work out the best solution for your school work. Do not be surprised or offended if you are asked to provide some proof that the tragedy is real. Many faculty members can be helpful and understanding when you're faced with this kind of situation, but they have a right to know for sure that they are not being taken advantage of. It is unfortunately true that an astonishing number of grandmothers seem to die around final exam time.

Coping With Academic Crises

The "Overload" Syndrome

Most colleges define a **full load** for you. This is the number of courses, or units, the faculty think a full-time student without any special problems can handle. In most programs, whether you're on the quarter system, semester system, or trimester system, the full load is set up so the average full-time student can finish the requirements for the bachelor's degree in four years. If a student takes more courses or more units than recommended for the full load, it's called an **overload**. Students who work hard, have excellent study skills, and few other demands on them can often handle more than a normal load, but too many students who sign up for overloads don't fit this description. They may be transfer students trying to make up required courses or people who are trying to get through in less than four years to save money.

For many of these students, signing up for an overload is one of the biggest mistakes they'll make. When you have one too many courses, it's not just the extra course that is hurt. You might be a solid "B" student with five courses. With a sixth course, you may always be behind and just scrape by in all your classes. One extra semester or quarter is not a large price to pay for doing well. If you must hurry, there are other ways to do it. For example, you might take a night course during the summer at a local community college, attend summer school, or take fewer courses with a larger number of units per course.

"Sophomore Slump"

A lot of students find their grades go down in their sophomore year. This doesn't happen to everyone, and there are many reasons for it—but it can be very depressing if it happens to you. Sometimes the reason is that you aren't as excited and/or scared as you were your first year, so you don't work as hard as you once did. Sometimes it happens because you are depressed about the breakup of your freshman romance. Also, many students who started college at 18 will be sophomores at an age when many people begin to wonder who they are and where they're going (the "identity crisis"). Demands from your college that you pick a major don't help either. A final reason for the slump is probably that courses are harder your sophomore year. You aren't taking all introductory courses anymore, and a new, more sophisticated kind of work is being asked of you (see Chapter 5 on writing papers and essay exams).

Whatever the reason for your sophomore slump, if you have one it may help to remember that it's called the *sophomore* slump because it usually goes away by the next year—but not by itself. You will have to pull yourself together and figure out what is wrong, possibly with the help of an adviser or counselor. You may learn how to do the new kind of work, or you might find a new romance. You may find out who you are and what you stand for, or you may just gradually stop thinking about it.

If finding out who you are is your problem, we've gathered a few suggestions other people have found helpful. It sometimes helps to make a list to assist you in figuring out your guiding principles. You can work from extreme examples—are you for or against child abuse and the torture of animals—up to more controversial points such as whether you would serve in the military if drafted. Conversations with friends can help you pin down your own ideas, ideas you may not have known you had until you heard a different point of view. Another approach is to think about the children you may someday have — what could they do that would shock and horrify you to the core? What things would you want them to believe in? What would you teach them to increase their chance for later happiness?

Just remember that in this process of personal discovery you cannot neglect your course work without having it show up in your grades. Too many poor grades may keep you from carrying out the plans you make. Your goal is to get back in control of your life. You want to get into courses that excite you, to learn new study techniques, to keep your personal life from running all over your work life. If you have a sophomore (or junior) slump it is another problem to be looked at, taken apart, and coped with. Just because a lot of people have it doesn't mean there's nothing you can do about it.

Probation

Most colleges and universities require students to maintain a minimum grade point average, usually somewhere around a C or a C–. Typically, a low grade in one course can be balanced out by a high grade in another. If your average drops below the minimum, you may be placed on **academic probation**. This is a warning that if your grades do not improve a lot the next semester, you may be dismissed from the college ("kicked out"). You should see probation as a second chance. The college is telling you something; you would not be on probation if you were doing things right.

If you find yourself on probation the first thing to do is to sit down and try to figure out how you should *change* what you have been doing. Your first job is to get off probation. The way to do it is to raise your grade average. Therefore, choose courses you can expect to do well in, and this does not mean you should sign up for Mickey Mouse courses. It does mean you should enroll in classes that have a lot of structure (courses that make you spread your work out over the whole term, for example, with a lot of quizzes). If you find yourself in trouble in any course, discuss it with the professor as soon as possible. S/he may be able to make some suggestions about how to study or give you some tips for that course. You can also get more general help from your academic adviser or the campus undergraduate office.

Flunking Out

Many students fail to keep their grades up to the minimum standards and are dismissed from a college. A common reason is that the student let course work go while concentrating on other problems (e.g., relationships, a job, drugs). Another is that the student does not have the appropriate study skills to do college work. In all these cases, there is generally something positive you can do if you still want a college education.

The first thing to do is to try to deal with whatever the main problem is. Perhaps your job takes too many hours a week. Most people cannot hold down two jobs and go to school, too. If you tried to do this and failed, the alternative is to consider a loan or work for a couple of years and save enough money to reduce the amount you have to work while going to school. Maybe the problem lies in your study habits. If reading Chapter 4 on study skills and Chapter 6 on managing your time is not enough, go to the library and read other books for ideas. Look into remedial reading and writing courses as additional sources of help.

Once you have isolated the major problem or problems that caused you to flunk out and have started working on a solution, then it's time to consider reapplying (although this is not always allowed) or applying to a different college, possibly one with lower standards. If you simply go from one college to another without *first* clearly facing the problem, your chances of failing a second time will be high.

Maybe College Isn't Right for You

There are other common reasons for flunking out (or, for that matter, hanging in but not doing very well). Some people just do not have the particular set of talents or interests that college requires. Just as some people could not easily be turned into good carpenters, cab drivers, athletes, inventors, and so forth, some cannot easily be turned into successful students. If your talents or interests do not match what is available in college, look elsewhere. There are technical schools, vocational schools, and on-the-job training programs to choose from. Many of these lead to careers that have as many challenges and pay as well (or better!) as those available to people with college degrees.

Flunking out of college—when it isn't the right place for you—can be a blessing in disguise if it prompts you to discover what your real interests and talents are. Would you be happier being the best auto mechanic in town or the worst high school teacher? For many students, the period after they flunk out is the first time they really sit down and consider what they like and don't like, what they are good at and what they find difficult, and what kind of day-to-day life they'd like to live.

Stopping Out

Suppose you are a good student but arrived at college with unrealistic and romantic expectations about the "pursuit of knowledge" or what your professors or fellow students would be like. You are disappointed, unchallenged, and drifting. Or, suppose college is pretty much what you expected, but you really only came to please your parents; you couldn't think of anything else to do, and now most of the time you are not at all interested in your course work, and you don't really feel like doing anything at all. Or, suppose you love school but can't seem to successfully juggle personal relationships and academic demands; everything is always falling apart, and you think you might be getting an ulcer.

These may be reasons to think about "**stopping out**" for a while — taking a year or two off from school to work or to get out on your own. While some students smoothly breeze through 4 years of college right after 12 years of elementary, junior high, and high school, others run out of steam and need to "recharge." Some students easily figure out who they are and where they are going at college, and others develop more self-control and self-confidence by meeting the daily demands of a full-time job. Whatever the reason, students who leave for a while and then decide to come back to college often do so with a clearer idea of their goals. What seemed hard before stopping out (e.g., budgeting time, seeing the relationship between studies and career goals) may seem easier afterward.

Further Thoughts on Coping

Obviously, no one could anticipate all the problems you might run into or, even if that were possible, suggest all the solutions that would work for you. But there are some things it helps to remember when things go wrong. It usually doesn't mean the end of the world. It may seem like it, but keeping a problem in perspective is an important step in dealing with it. Try to consider priorities — some things can't be ignored, and others can wait. Learning to tell the difference continues throughout your life. Sometimes you make mistakes — through ignorance or through a gamble. If it was ignorance, being better informed will prevent a mistake next time. If it was a gamble, lose gracefully. If you bet there wouldn't be a surprise quiz the next day and went to the party instead of studying, don't flounce around in class if you guessed wrong.

With the "big problems," beware of self-absorption. It is tempting for all of us to feel like nobody has troubles like ours, but look around you. No matter how complex your problem or situation, try to analyze it. Take it apart and find some part of it, however small, that you might be able to solve or make better. Take yourself in hand if you need to. Don't make other people responsible for you. Do ask others for help. Asking for help is very different from making someone else responsible for you. Share your problems (and ideas for solutions) with a friend. When you need it, seek information from books or people who might be able to help you. Using available resources for help when you need it is one of the smartest things you can do. Problems are a natural and inevitable part of life. Learning how to cope with them creatively is a skill that grows with practice.

9.

Away or at Home: Where Should You Live?

There are a lot of different kinds of living arrangements, each with its strong and weak points. The purpose of this section is to alert you to some of the things you should keep in mind when considering where to live.

Away From Home

Suppose you've decided to go away to college. Where will you live when you get there?

On Campus

Campus Dormitory

The dorm is typically the most convenient and almost always the best for freshmen. You're right there, close to the library, close to your classes. A dormitory involves community living, either on a hall or in a suite, using community bathrooms and laundry facilities and eating in a cafeteria. On some campuses, dorms may be "coed" (people of both sexes live in the same dorm and may share some facilities including the bathrooms). One big advantage, besides being near your daily activities, is that the dorm is a fast way to meet a lot of people. You also learn your way around the campus and hear about campus activities quickly. Transportation is no problem, and you don't have much responsibility for upkeep.

Of course, there are drawbacks (of more or less importance depending on your personality). The personal space is very limited, and you won't have much privacy. Usually dormitory rooms are shared with one or two other people. How you and your roommate get along is very important (see pages 126-128). Roommates can be changed, but it's hard to do this in the middle of a term. Some campuses have single rooms available, usually for a higher fee, but because the number is limited, single rooms often are not available to first-year students.

Off Campus

Sororities and Fraternities

Some campuses have sororities (women) and fraternities (men). These are groups of people who live and eat together, work on group projects both for the campus and the community, and arrange social events. They often have names that are letters of the Greek alphabet, for example, Alpha Delta. Some of these organizations are nationwide and have "chapters" at a number of different campuses. To join, you usually have to be invited to do so by the group.

At their best, these groups create a lot of group spirit and provide a way for students to help each other with the social and academic pressures of college. Some sororities and fraternities have, for example, a rule that members must keep their grades up to a certain level, and advanced students often tutor others who are having problems.

At their worst, sororities and fraternities expect too much conformity from members, create "cliques," and may encourage racial or religious prejudice. Students may begin to feel that being invited to join one of the "better" groups is terribly important as a sign of a person's social value. New members, called "pledges," usually go through some kind of "hazing," where older members of the group ask them to do silly things. Unfortunately, students occasionally are asked to do some things that result in serious injury, so be sure to always use your own judgment.

Whether sororities and fraternities help students avoid pressures or actually add new ones depends on the group and the campus.

Room in a Private House

Some people in the community around a campus rent rooms in their homes to students. This may provide you with a quieter environment than the average dorm and perhaps more privacy, depending on your landlord or landlady. It's harder to develop a sense of belonging to the campus community when you are living by yourself, though, and you will have the problem of transportation to solve if the house is not within walking distance of the campus. If you tend to be a "loner" and don't want to be, this is probably the wrong choice for you.

Apartment

Most students will have to share an apartment with other people in order to afford it. An apartment may give you a place that feels a little more like your own home. It may be a quieter place to study and a more private place than a dorm or a room in a private home. However, in an apartment you do not have control over your neighbors, and whether or not the apartment is really better for studying and sleeping than the dorm will depend partly on the habits and courtesy of your neighbors. A building full of other students is likely to have more noise than one full of people who have to get up and go to work. On the other hand, a building full of students may be more sympathetic to the noise you make. Also, you're very likely to spend more time cleaning and perhaps cooking in an apartment than you would in a dorm, and of course you should take into account whether transportation will be a problem.

Sharing a House

An increasingly popular living arrangement is for a group of students to get together and rent a house. This often has a more home-like atmosphere with more living space than, for example, a dorm room. To afford a house you probably will need more roommates, and of course, the more people around, the more likely it is you will be bothered by noise. A house also involves many more responsibilities than any other living arrangement. In addition to cooking and cleaning, you'll have to take care of the place. You will have to put out the garbage cans, water and mow the lawn, call the plumber or electrician when problems occur, and arrange to be home when service people come (and because they usually won't be tied down to a specific time, this can waste whole days). Someone may have to sign a lease and be legally responsible for the whole rent, even if a housemate skips town. On the other hand, if the owner doesn't want a lease, it means that s/he can kick you out on short notice.

Some Further Thoughts About Living Off-Campus

For any off-campus living arrangement, you should look into the availability of public transportation. Try to live close to public transportation even if you have a car. You don't want to miss important exams or lectures because your car is being repaired and you can't get to school. If you don't enjoy food shopping and cooking, consider buying a meal plan even though you live off-campus. It is often possible to have your own apartment and still eat on campus at a dorm. And finally, as a general rule, don't get involved in an apartment or a house lease with people you don't know. A good group of people can be like a family, and a bad group of people can be a miserable experience.

Turning Strangers Into Family

In any living arrangement, whether it is a dorm, an apartment, or a house, people can do things to make it pleasant and successful and to cut down on arguments. Sit down with your roommate or housegroup early on

to discuss the kinds of things that will require cooperation. Will you leave the doors locked or unlocked? Will you share food or can you count on that box of crackers being there when you get back? Will there be "quiet" hours? Should others be asked before guests are invited? Should friends be told to call before they come by or do you want to encourage dropping in? What about cleaning? Who's going to do what?

Take some initiative in organizing a discussion with your roommate(s). It can be hard to change roommates, and it may be simpler to compromise or agree to disagree than to find a totally compatible roommate, especially your freshman year. We knew a compulsive cleaner and a slob who shared a room happily for a year by running a strip of masking tape down the center.

Increasingly, the responsibility for making the living arrangement work belongs to students. Twenty years ago almost every campus dormitory had very specific rules of conduct. These rules covered things such as how loud record players could be and when there could be no noise at all (quiet hours). In the women's dorms, the hours when men could visit were rigidly controlled, and the outer doors to the building were locked soon after the library closed on weekday nights and a little later on weekends. Rooms were inspected for neatness. Often there was a dorm judiciary committee, made up of students, that gave out penalties if you broke rules, for example, if you didn't get in before the doors were locked.

Today, many campuses are reluctant to set living rules for students. This, of course, allows more freedom for individuals. However, if a group fails to agree on rules, the living situation can be very unpleasant. It may be impossible to study because of the noise. There may be mice and roaches everywhere because food isn't wrapped up. Whatever the problem, the group should get together and discuss a solution. Better yet, get together to discuss these issues before a problem comes up. One important point the group should consider is that not locking the outside doors makes it more likely that personal property will be stolen and assaults and rapes will take place. If you can't get cooperation and intelligent discussion from your group on really important issues, you should consider looking for a new group.

Problems can develop in any living situation, but cooperation in solving problems can often be gotten by giving it. Don't wait for somebody else.

Survival Skills

While college is designed to teach you lots of new ideas, techniques, and ways of thinking out problems, there are a few things you should be sure you know before you arrive. They're not the sort you'll find included in the courses you're taking, and you may already be an expert in some or all of them. We mention them, though, because they are often overlooked. Quite simply, they are *survival* skills.

You should be prepared to open a checking account and know how to write checks and balance a checkbook. You should know how to use a coin-operated laundromat. What kinds of clothing can you wash together in the same load without all of them coming out blue, purple, or pink? How much soap should you put in? How high should you set the dryer? What can be dried without shrinking or melting? You don't need many clothes and as many of them as possible should be drip dry, but you should know how to iron.

You should know how to use a stove and how to cook a few simple, inexpensive things. This is probably a good idea even if you're going to be in a dorm with a meal plan. Somebody with a kitchen might invite you over, and chances are you'll be expected to pitch in. You should know some basic housekeeping—how to change the vacuum cleaner bag, how to make a bed, why you clean wood furniture with a rag and polish rather than soap and water. You should also know how to type. If you don't, buy a typing manual and start practicing or arrange to take some lessons.

Of course, many people reading this book already know how to do all these things, but many others, and a surprising number at that, don't know how to do one or more of them. We didn't know how to do all of these things our first term. Don't be embarrassed. Ask somebody. Ask your parents, a friend, an older brother or sister. Find someone to help you and learn how to do what you don't already know. You can wait until you get to college, but it's usually easier to have these survival skills in advance.

Something else you might want to think about is how you handle your finances. We feel it is a good idea to take on at least some financial responsibility. Many of you have no choice. You have worked hard to save the money to go to college, or you'll be working while you're in college. But even if you are being helped by your parents or other relatives or friends, you can still share in managing your financial affairs. Many students follow a budget and keep track of when bills are due, for example, various college fees, car insurance payments, and dormitory bills.

What Should You Take With You?

You shouldn't need a moving van. Make your motto "travel light."

Household

How much household equipment you'll need depends, of course, on whether you are renting or sharing a house, staying in the dorm, living in an apartment, etc. Minimum equipment no matter where you live is a cup, glass, can opener, plate, bowl, knife, fork, and spoon. Also take a supply of containers or plastic bags to tie up crackers or cookies, so that your midnight snacks won't attract mice and roaches.

If you will be living in a dorm, find out if you are expected to bring sheets, blankets, bedspread, or towels, or whether they will be provided for you. There may be an optional linen service for an extra fee. You might want to hold off on those giant stereo speakers and your TV set until you see what your roommate has brought, how much room you have, what the dorm noise rules are, and how safe your possessions will be from theft. In any event, don't bring valuable jewelry or anything else you would hate to lose.

Clothes

You won't need closets full of clothes, but you will need hangers for what you do bring. Depending on where you live, you may not have a whole closet to yourself, anyway. The type of everyday clothing you'll wear will depend on the college or university you have selected. Styles vary, and so do climates.

It is a good idea to have one set of old clothes and one set of "going out" clothes, but mostly you'll need everyday clothes that are *easy to care for*. One solution is to take a few comfortable clothes you already have and wait until you get to college to see if you need anything else. If you want to buy some things in advance, pictures in college catalogs or information you picked up visiting the campus should give you some idea of what other students are wearing. But remember, the heavy coats available in stores in Alabama may not hold up under a Maine winter, and the fall clothes sold in North Dakota may not be ideal for a Texas climate. Also, a few colleges have a dress code, so be sure to check on this ahead of time.

Tools of the Trade

Items you should be sure to bring are a desk lamp with several extra bulbs, a dictionary, a thesaurus, a typewriter (even if it's only a garage sale special), and depending on what courses you expect to take, a pocket or desk calculator. You'll also want to have an alarm clock, preferably the wind-up kind, so that you can get to class on time even if there is a power failure!

Living at Home

There are many different reasons why students who have a choice live with their families and commute to college. Most younger students who choose to live at home do so to save money. If a college with the right program is close by, commuting can be a good way to cut down on the cost of a college education. Family responsibilities are another common reason students commute, especially for older or returning students. Still other students are comfortable at home and are reluctant to leave. This section is for you if you are, or are thinking about becoming, a college commuter. Whatever your reasons for commuting to college, there are special advantages, and problems, that you may face compared with others who are living away from home.

Living With Parents—Pros and Cons

A major advantage to living at home with parents is that the transition from high school to college is usually a bit smoother. Freshmen living away from home many for the first time find themselves facing a lot of problems with everyday living. Dealing with a roommate, for example, can take time and be stressful at first. Few students are lucky enough to be matched up from the start with roommates who like and dislike all of the same things they do. Early risers get paired with night owls; neat people with messy ones; talkative, outgoing people with shy, silent types. Working out a living arrangement that is satisfying to all parties takes time and energy. During your freshman year you won't have much of either to spare.

Living without familiar faces (not to mention home cooking) can also be hard at first. The family and friends who saw you through so much before are no longer there everyday to share your joys and sorrows. Freshmen away from home for the first time are often lonely and homesick. Finally, being totally on your own generally makes you responsible for more details of your day-to-day life than when you live at home — taking care of them takes time and planning. When all of these personal changes are added to new and harder course work, the problems may seem great.

These points in favor of commuting, though, can also be seen as points against it. Many people argue that college is a time for personal as well as intellectual growth, and that no one can really grow until they move away from home. This, of course, is too general a statement to apply to everyone, and it is clearly false in some cases. Problems can come up, though, when neither parent nor child sees the need to change patterns they are used to.

Personal Growth

Just what do we mean by "personal growth"? The term is one of those that most people understand but find hard to define. Basically, it means all those things that go into making someone an independent person, able to act and enjoy life away from his or her family. It includes feeling that you can cope with problems as they come up, being responsible for details of daily living like housekeeping and shopping and believing you are able to make both the big and little decisions that are a part of your life.

Families differ a lot in how much they help you to learn to do things. Perhaps it's worth thinking about your own family. Frequently, while they make a warm, comfortable home for you, parents also protect you too much and don't expect you to be responsible for much except cleaning your room once in a while. You are the best judge of your own home. Try to think about it as an outsider would and decide what, if anything, you would like to change to help you become more independent.

We suggest that, if possible, you pay part of the cost of your living expenses, whether or not your family needs the money. This often gives both parents and children a new outlook about each other. Many undergraduates living away from home in dorms never do this. By not taking some responsibility for their living expenses, they are missing an important part of their personal growth. Taking charge of more of the everyday details of your life is also a step that can be taken slowly while still living at home. Offer to cook once in a while. Do your own laundry.

Adjusting to Your New Life

One difficulty faced by commuters is that parents, brothers, sisters, spouses, and children are often not aware of how much a new college student has to do. You may have sailed through high school. Even so, you could still find yourself pressed for time in college and sometimes overwhelmed by it all. You need more space, time, and peace and quiet than ever before, although you may be the only one who knows it. The best way to solve this problem is to deal with it as directly and as early as possible. Sit down and discuss your problems and needs with the family. You can't expect life to stop in your house because you've started college, but you might reach compromises on important points. Talk about things openly and rationally. Yelling probably won't work, and even if it does, it hardly fits with the "new you" you are trying to build.

Getting Involved

Commuting students sometimes say they don't really feel like a part of their campuses — they feel like visitors. This is a frequent problem, but one that fortunately has a fairly straightforward solution. As we shall see, it is straightforward but not necessarily easy. In a word, the solution is *involvement*.

It is easy to arrive on campus, go to classes, and then hop in your car or on the bus for the ride home. It's harder to find people to talk to after class or to join a club or a volunteer tutoring group. While living on campus does not guarantee that a student will do these things, it does make it easier. As a commuter, you'll have to go out of your way a bit more, but it's well worth it.

Look out for and make friends with other commuters (there may even be a commuter club). They may be people you'd want to know anyway, and you'll be able to talk about the problems you share. It's always good to learn that you are not the only one with a problem, and that there are ways of dealing with it. However, don't *only* make friends with commuters. You don't have to live on campus to be friendly with those who do. People who don't live in dorms often go to dormitory activities as guests of people who do live there — a Friday afternoon beer bash, for example. It is also especially valuable to meet people who are different from you in ethnic or socioeconomic background, but as a commuter, you may have to actively look for them.

Getting There

One more problem for commuters is "How do I get there?" You need reliable transportation. Whether you provide your own (e.g., car) or use public transportation (e.g., bus or train), be prepared for problems. Some you will have no control over (a sudden flat tire or late train) but try to build some extra time into your schedule. Also, you can do things to keep disaster from happening in the first place.

Keep your car in good shape. If the battery is weak, replace it. If you say a little prayer every time you turn the key, perhaps it is time to replace the starter, too. The extra money will seem small compared to saving yourself the aggravation of not knowing when or if you will arrive on campus.

If the weather is bad, particularly if it is snowing, allow extra time to get where you are going. Trains almost always run late in the snow, and cars get stuck. Build these possibilities into your thinking. Students often give problems like these as an excuse for missing or coming late to an exam. Faculty members have different feelings about this; many are not very sympathetic and think you should have planned better. The best bet is to make it less likely that these things will happen.

Parking

Somewhere there is probably a campus with lots of commuter parking next to each building and excellent signs and maps to help you find the right lot. Unfortunately we don't know where this wonderful college is, and the chances are your college parking situation will be a lot less pleasant. Parking for commuters is often so difficult and mixed up that we recommend you visit the campus to find out about it before classes start. Visit the campus parking office if there is one (call before to find out) or campus security (police). You may need a sticker to park on campus. You may only be allowed to park in certain lots with the rest being saved for faculty, staff, or dorm students. You may have to park so far from class that you'll have to take a ten-minute bus ride to the center of campus. Find out how often these buses are supposed to run, how often they really run, and then allow still more time, especially during the first weeks and on exam or bad-weather days.

Is there a pay parking garage? Find out which parking offenses get you tickets (perhaps parking without a sticker) and which get you towed (e.g., parking in a handicapped space or a fire lane). Find out where your car will be towed to, how much and how (cash? check?) you'll have to pay to get it back, and what hours the towing yard is open. Find out how the college collects on tickets (by not letting you register for next term? by not letting you graduate?). If you take a train, find out where you can park at the station and how far from campus and what connections there are at the other end. And remember, lots that were vacant before classes start may be jammed when college opens.

Finally, never, never park in a handicapped space. No one gets a handicapped parking sticker unless s/he really needs it. You may think you see able-bodied people parking with these stickers, but not all handicaps show (e.g., heart defects, artificial legs). Or, that person you saw may be an attendant going in to pick up a paraplegic student.

Should I Commute?

The reasons students commute are so different, and students themselves are so different, it would be impossible for us to give a general answer to the question, "Should I commute?" By pointing out some things to consider, however, we have tried to give you the information you'll need to reach the right answer for you.

In some situations, there is no choice—the student must commute. You do, though, have the choice of how much you get out of it. In other cases, you may get to decide whether or not to commute. Our suggestion is to make up a list of the advantages and disadvantages to both commuting and living away from home. Often when you've spelled it out, the right choice for you will be clear. The important thing to remember is that whether or not you get a lot out of college doesn't depend on where you live.

10.

Tips for the Two-Year College Student

Maybe you are a student who wants a college education but are not ready to make the commitment to four more years of school, or perhaps you are older, with a family, returning to school after many years. You may have learned that your career goals require two years of technical training, or your grades may not have been high enough to get you into a four-year college right out of high school. These are just a few of the many reasons why you may be one of the five-million students in the United States attending a two-year college.

How much of this book applies to you if you are in a two-year college? The answer is "just about everything." Our advice on study skills, dealing with faculty, personal problems, etc., holds for every student. Why, then, a separate chapter on two-year colleges? The answer is simple. There are a few *extra* facts, hints, tips, and pieces of advice we'd like to share with you. We think they will help you get the most out of school.

What Is a Two-Year College?

Two-year colleges come in three basic forms. The first, often called a "junior" college, primarily offers the first two years of undergraduate work. Some students may then transfer to a four-year college for their junior and senior years. These colleges, which may be privately or publicly operated, offer Associate of Arts (A.A.) and Associate of Science (A.S.) degrees. These programs involve courses like those you would be taking as a freshman or sophomore at a four-year school, for example, English, math, history, biology. Not everyone at a junior college plans to transfer, however, and many attend with the A.A. or A.S. degree as their final goal.

The second type of two-year college is the technical or vocational college or institute. These schools usually offer A.S. degrees in a number of applied areas such as medical technology, electronics, and dental hygiene. While students in these programs take courses in basic academic fields as well, emphasis is placed on applied work to enable graduates to enter their chosen career right out of school.

The third type of two-year college is the comprehensive school that offers both kinds of programs we've just described. Since they are almost always publicly run and supported at least in part by local tax money, they are often called "community colleges."

Students at all of these two-year colleges usually live at home or off campus since this type of school rarely has dormitories.

Pluses and Minuses

Perhaps you think of two-year colleges as simply a continuation of high school. While they are much more than that, it's true that high schools and two-year colleges have more in common than high schools and four-year colleges. These similarities result in both advantages and disadvantages. You should know about them so that you can get the most out of the positives and work to avoid the negatives.

On the Plus Side

Smaller Classes

Introductory courses at most four-year colleges tend to be large, and in some cases can be quite large, for example, several hundred students. This rarely happens in a two-year college. Classes are usually small, perhaps 25 students or less, and there may be more opportunity to participate in discussions and to ask questions. (Class size in general is discussed further in the Appendix.)

More Personal Attention

Because classes are smaller, instructors in two-year colleges can spend more time helping individual students, both in and out of class. Also, most two-year college teachers are not under pressure to publish (see Chapter 3) or do research as are many professors at four-year schools; this means they can spend more of their time at the college teaching. (The Appendix describes how faculty members at different types of colleges use their time.)

Lower Cost

Two-year colleges are usually much less expensive than four-year in-stitutions. Not only are fees much lower, but a great deal is saved by living at home and commuting to school. At the present time, the average cost for tuition and living expenses at public four-year colleges is $4000 per year, while the figure for private colleges is $7000 per year. Since many two-year college courses are offered in the evening as well as during the day, it can be easier to work full or part time and still go to school.

Easier Adjustment

Because students usually go to a two-year college near their home, the adjustment to school can be easier than that at a four-year college away from home. It isn't necessary to become familiar with an entirely new community and to "start out from scratch." Also, two-year colleges are usually smaller and tend to be less overwhelming for a new student. It can be easier to find your way around—both academically and socially.

More Opportunity to Explore Career Choices

Two-year colleges can give students a greater opportunity to look into different careers while they are still students. The advising staff is usually very helpful and knowledgeable about career options, and two-year colleges typically offer a wide variety of career-oriented courses to choose from. Regardless of whether you plan to transfer later or go right into a job, this chance to find out what you are interested in can be extremely valuable.

Greater Diversity Among Students

While the student body at most four-year colleges is becoming more and more diverse each year, most of the students are still 18–23-year-olds who enroll right out of high school. Two-year colleges, on the other hand, are a

THERE'S A GREAT DIVERSITY AMONG STUDENTS.

real mix of younger and older students from different backgrounds. These people will bring their wide range of experiences to the classroom and can contribute different viewpoints and perspectives. This can make learning, both in and out of the classroom, more interesting and help prepare you for life outside of school.

Some Possible Pitfalls

As you might have guessed, there are some possible disadvantages to a two-year college. Knowing that they exist, though, can help you avoid or minimize them.

Personal Growth May Be Harder

Two-year college students fresh out of high school are usually not faced with the same kinds of adjustments that their friends in four-year colleges are. Since you are probably living at home, you have the day-to-day support of family and old friends, and it is easy to continue doing things in the same way you've always done them. Also, two-year colleges tend to have more services to assist students, and less responsibility is placed on students as a result.

Both kinds of support work together against developing independence and new outlooks, unless you actively work to achieve them. Pages 131–134 of Chapter 9, dealing with the special problems of growing up while still living at home, make some suggestions we think are very useful.

Less Challenge

Since two-year colleges usually do not admit students on the basis of grades, a typical class will have students who differ widely in ability. Instructors have varying ways of dealing with the problem: some aim for the middle of the road, others attempt to teach at a pace so that even the weakest student can keep up, and still others seem to pay little attention to the ability of the students and concentrate only on the material.

If you want more challenging courses, find out about who gives the type of course you are looking for by asking around. If you find yourself in a course that is too slow for you, you might ask the instructor for extra supplementary work. Seek out the best students for informal, after-class talks. With a little effort on your part, your classes can be what you want them to be.

Lower Morale

Some students at two-year colleges start out with a self-defeating attitude. This is particularly true of students who would prefer to be at a four-year college but were unable to go, either because of their grades or their financial situation. They have the attitude that their classes will be second rate, and that it really doesn't matter how hard they work, they'll do well regardless.

This couldn't be further from the truth. Two-year college courses can be challenging and stimulating, and how well you do in them will determine not only whether you will be able to transfer to the four-year college of your choice or land that great job, but how much you will learn. Make the commitment to doing university-level work and stick to it.

What Kind of Program Do You Want?

In most two-year colleges, you must make an important choice soon after you arrive—or even before enrollment. Do you want the pretransfer program or do you want a program tied to a particular career ("career," "vocational," or "terminal" are some of the common names for this kind of program)? Courses are usually set up so that it will take two years of full-time study to finish either the pretransfer or the career program, if you go straight through. Because of this, the college usually wants to know fairly soon what you are doing, and so do you. In the next sections we will talk about these two choices in more detail, but you should remember that there is a third choice as well. It's not against the law to waver or change your mind. It may take you a while longer to finish if you do change, but that's much better than winding up in something you're not happy with.

Special Problems and Benefits of Pre-Career Programs

There are many kinds of career programs from dental assistant to fire science. Not all two-year colleges offer every one. If you have a clear idea of what you want, and it's not offered at the nearest school, it may make sense to commute further to be able to get your first choice.

Make the Choice That's Right for You

The Issue of Prestige. A problem for many vocational students is a feeling that such programs have less prestige than pretransfer programs. This is obviously related to the fact that the careers you can choose with an A.S. degree have less glamour in many people's eyes than those you can choose with more advanced degrees. A dental hygienist has less prestige than a dentist. It's not only a matter of money; mechanics make more money than college professors in most states but have less prestige. The reasons why different occupations have different levels of prestige are often not clear, nor are the reasons why some jobs pay more than others.

If this doesn't bother you in terms of your career planning—if you wouldn't be a dentist if they paid you double—then you shouldn't let it bother you at college. If it does bother you, then you may have chosen the wrong career. You want one you like so much that you don't care what other people say, and one that you'd do even if it paid less.

Look at All the Opportunities.   In choosing a career program, don't just pick one because it seems like a "natural" thing to do, or because it is the only thing you know about. Take some time to find out about a number of potential careers. Attend field trips to businesses and government agencies that are held by some community colleges in cooperation with local employers. Talk to other students about what they are going to do and why. Ask the reference librarian for information about various jobs and visit the career counseling center and take any tests that are available. If you can, take basic courses leading to more than one career.

Find out about the average pay in various careers and the opportunities for advancement. For example, you could start out studying electronics with the hope of eventually having your own business.

Also, find out as much as you can about the working conditions and what people in that career actually spend their time on. This will not only help you decide whether this is the career for you but also give you some ideas about what extra courses you might take.

All this looking and thinking is worth the trouble. You may discover one or two careers that are more attractive to you than what you had in mind when you started. Or you may discover a career that is equally as good for your interests and talents, but that has better working conditions, higher pay, or more opportunity for advancement.

Teaching (and Learning) Style

Generally, no matter what career program you choose, you will have to take a few liberal arts courses (perhaps basic English, history, or math courses). In some colleges, the liberal arts and vocational faculty have different styles of teaching and testing. Moving from one type of course to the other can be tough. Conversations with other students will give you some idea of how true this is in your school. Since you must pass both the vocational and liberal arts courses to get your vocational degree, it will pay for you to notice these differences and figure out how to deal with them.

One difference is that professors in the vocational courses often teach about immediately useful things (or at least about things that can be applied as soon as you start your career). Liberal arts courses are more likely to be about theories and ideas and may not appear to be as practical. Of course, you often learn useful ideas in a liberal arts course (e.g., when to use what kind of punishment may be discussed in your child development course), and sometimes you learn theory in a vocational course (e.g., you may be taught theories of electricity in a wiring course), but usually there is more practical information in a vocational course than in a liberal arts class.

If you are a very practical person it may be hard to stay interested in a liberal arts area. It may help you to realize, though, that each theory has different recommendations or advice to give about practical situations. This may give you more interest in finding out which theory is best. For instance, different theories of punishment and reward suggest different methods of child rearing. A history or political science course can make you a more informed voter. Your liberal arts professors will probably be glad to talk about the implications and recommendations of different theories and ideas, if you ask.

Planning to Transfer After Two Years?

If you've decided to transfer after finishing your two-year degree, there are some things you should keep in mind so the transition will go smoothly.

What Courses Should I Take?

When planning your pretransfer program at a two-year college, keep in mind that you'll want to be able to get **transfer credit** for as many of the courses as possible. Transfer credit means that your new school will count the credits you've already earned toward your four-year degree. Advisers at your two-year school should be able to help you select wisely.

Introductory courses in different fields are usually good choices, since they are easily transferred and tend to be the largest classes at four-year schools. By taking them now, you'll have the benefit of smaller classes, and you'll begin to get some ideas about possible majors. Save advanced courses until after you transfer so you can get to know the professors at your new college in small classes. You will need to know professors well so that they can write personal recommendations for jobs or graduate school.

On the other hand, you may be interested in certain technical areas, such as accounting, welding, or computer programming, that may not be offered at the college you plan to transfer to. In this case, you might want to take a few relevant courses while you have the opportunity. The credits may not transfer, but what you learn may be well worth your time.

Other courses that probably aren't transferable are remedial courses in English and mathematics. If you are weak in these areas, don't let concern about losing credit keep you from building up your skills. You can always go to summer school to pick up extra credits if you are worried about falling behind because you took remedial classes. You will be much better off in your four-year college if you come prepared with a good background in reading, writing, and math, regardless of whether you'll be given transfer credit for the courses you took to get these skills.

Be Involved

While you are at your two-year college, take advantage of the different kinds of activities available outside of your classes. Join clubs, participate in sports, attend social and cultural activities. Doing these things will make you feel more involved in your college and will help you get more out of it. If you get into the habit of participating at your two-year college, you'll probably continue to be an active student once you transfer.

Choosing a Four-Year College

You should do some thinking about the kind of four-year college you want. They may all look the same from where you are, but if you do well in your two-year college, you will have a choice. In some states, if you complete your program with a certain average (which may be D, C, or B depending on the state), there is usually a state-supported four-year college that *must* accept you as a transfer student. This can be a good choice if the college offers the kinds of courses you are interested in. Many students also apply to private institutions or other public colleges, either in their home state or away. Talk to an adviser at your two-year college and read some of the many books that deal with the programs and requirements at different schools. (Read the Appendix of this book to get a general overview of the things to look for.)

Money

Many students at community colleges do not know how much a year at a four-year institution can cost. If you are commuting to a community college your expenses may be very, very low. Transferring to the nearest branch of the state university and living there will probably cost you several thousand dollars more a year. A private college will be even more expensive. While financial aid may be available, it rarely covers all the costs at a four-year college. The increased expense should not discourage you, but you should start planning how to meet it now.

Dealing With Change

Your first term at a four-year college will very likely be a definite change from your old school. The differences may be in registration routines, class sizes, the kind of work required, or reduced personal attention. An important difference is that while you may have done very well at your old school and been the big fish in a small pond, at your new college you will be with other people just like yourself. Either they will be other people who did well in a two-year college, or they will be people who did well in high school and have already been at your new college for two years.

You will have to work harder with this new competition at the same time that you are adjusting to your new college's requirements and ways of doing things. Most transfers find that their grades go down somewhat (a half grade) their first term. If you work hard and adjust, they will go back up, but it takes time.

Another problem is that just as you are having to get used to all these changes in your academic life, you are also getting used to changes in your personal life. For many transfer students, their junior year is the first time they've ever lived away from home. All the personal support you are used to from both family and friends has suddenly disappeared. On the other hand, though, you are at least two years older than you would have been as a freshman and are probably better able to cope than you would have been then.

There are some things you can do to make these changes easier. To find out what the school is really like, visit the campus while class is in session. Meet people and talk to departmental advisers. Attend orientation meetings held especially for transfer students. Then your first day on campus will go more smoothly.

Once You're There

You may find it takes more effort to get what you want at a four-year college than it did at your two-year school. Don't let this discourage you. If you are used to a college that went out of its way to take care of you, a four-year school may seem much colder and more impersonal. In a short time, though, you can make the adjustment and get the benefits that go along with your new college. Get to know your classmates by being involved both in and out of class.

11.

Special Students With Special Problems

People can be different or feel different for a lot of reasons — physical, social, political, religious, etc. Although this chapter is written mainly for students who are different or special in ways they fear may make it harder for them to succeed academically (e.g., poorly prepared, handicapped, or returning to school after many years away), we have two pieces of advice that are good for *any* student who feels "different." In short, these are (1) find others like yourself for moral and practical help and support and (2) divide your time between this "support group" and the rest of the students who go to your college.

You need to spend time with people who are *not like you* because you need to learn how to be comfortable with them in the future. You also need to find and spend time with people *like* yourself. You can learn a great deal from them — many have been through problems similar to yours and have worked through them. No matter how unusual, lonely, or isolated you feel, you are not alone — there are almost certainly others on campus who would be willing to help if they knew you needed a hand.

Special Admissions—What Is It? Am I One?

At one time, most colleges chose students who were pretty much alike: everyone came from the same general background, had the same kind of grades, and knew the same kind of people. For years now, however, colleges have tried to enroll students from many varying backgrounds. For example, you might find that you and your roommates were all B + or A − students in high school, but that one of you went to a small country high school, one to a rundown overcrowded city high school, and one to an expensive private school. You all had good recommendations, but one of you averaged 500 on the SAT aptitude tests, one 400, and one 600. The idea is that students learn by meeting people who are different from themselves.

More recently, another goal has been to give a chance to students who might be able to do college work, but whose preparation for college is weak. This last group of students is the special admissions category, and this section of the chapter is about their problems.

If you had above-average SAT scores and above-average grades from a good high school, you are almost certainly a **general admissions** student. On the other hand, a **special admissions** student is more likely to have come from a small or poorly funded high school, one that did not give all the usual high school courses (e.g., language or upper-level mathematics). You may also be a special admissions student if you did not take or do well in certain basic courses. This means you don't know all the material other students know and will have to work hard to catch up. It also means, however, the faculty and administration think you can catch up if you try, and they may give special courses to help you.

Dealing With Your Problems

As a special admissions student you have two problems. One is you don't know the background material. The second is that it is hard to admit to yourself and to others that you don't know it. You have to solve the second problem before you can work on the first.

A lot of students with poor backgrounds feel that if they can't do calculus or college chemistry it means they're stupid. It helps most people to realize that no one can do calculus after one year of high school algebra. You may not have taken the right courses because your counselor didn't point them out to you or because they didn't seem important to you at the time or because your school didn't offer them. You may have taken them and failed. Of course, even if you have someone else to blame instead of yourself, you can't stop there. You are stuck with the problems of making up that extra work yourself. Even if it was your high school adviser's fault, s/he is not here to make up the work—you have to. The other students did it in high school while you were taking easier courses. Now you will have to work harder while these courses may be easier for them.

It may help a little to realize that this makeup time won't last forever, if you get started right away. If you don't get going, though, you will still feel lost your senior year—if you haven't already flunked out. Figure out what your problems are so you can work on them. The two most serious weaknesses are not being able to read and understand what you read quickly and not being able to write clearly. These problems will hurt your work in almost all college courses. If not solved during college, these problems will limit the jobs you can get as well as your promotions later on.

Some classes that might get left out entirely in high school are the kind that other courses build on: you may have arrived missing basic building blocks, such as math. Other classes are also important because you need them for many majors. If you never take college math, you will close off all but a few majors—and those remaining may not prepare you for the job or career you really want.

How do you go about making up what you are missing? If you are in an official special admissions program, talk to a counselor in that office before you come, or as soon as you arrive, about what your problems may be. They probably have special courses or tutors you can use, maybe even before the first term starts. If school has not started, you may find the course you want in a nearby high school summer program.

Special admissions counselors may see gaps in your training you don't know about. Listen to them. They have met other students with your problems and have seen who has succeeded and who has failed. If what your advisers are saying isn't clear, maybe they are being too tactful. Ask them to spell it out. If you are a special admissions student, there is a reason. The "special" means you are missing some preparation. Find out what.

The special admissions office or another office may offer courses on study techniques (also see Chapters 4, 5, and 6). There are several signals that you might need to learn something about how to study. Low grades in high school, of course, probably mean you haven't been doing it right. On the other hand, you may have had high grades in high school but took mostly easy courses. You develop the study skills you need for college in more difficult classes, not easy ones. Another place to get help may be from juniors or seniors in your program; they may have had and solved the same problems you now have.

English as a Second Language

Perhaps you are a special admissions student who does not speak English well. This may make you afraid to talk to faculty and other students; then you will spend too much time with your own ethnic group (and probably not studying). You will miss out on help you need from the faculty, and your English won't get better. Speak English *all* the time. Allow yourself Saturday night off perhaps, but you must practice your English. If you don't know how to speak, understand, and read and write English *well* in the United States, college will be a struggle. Also, there are many jobs that won't be open to you. On the other hand, if you speak English *and* another language, you will have many more choices.

Minorities

Many special admissions students are from racial or ethnic minorities and thus may have to deal with both open and hidden prejudice while they are coping with academic problems. They also face the sometimes difficult task of deciding when someone is discriminating against them and when someone just doesn't like them or something they do. Of course, how big a factor all this is depends on your school and whether you have friends (both from your ethnic group and outside it) to help you over the rough spots. Many schools have one or more advisers for helping minority students cope with discrimination or an active program that you might want to join to fight prejudice. In addition, there may be a club for members of your group that can provide suggestions for actions you can take as well as moral support. If you feel you will have particular problems, allow for the added strain when you plan your program; take a lighter load the first semester.

One aspect of this problem that is not so obvious is the damage done to minority students by their friends. Many professors feel very strongly about the past injustices suffered by different groups. A few express their understanding and sympathy by requiring less from minority students. You will quickly learn who is "sympathetic" and who is an easy grader. Try to resist the temptation to take most of your courses from such faculty, because they are *not* doing you a favor.

Faculty are there to help you learn what you don't know. If you are passing or getting good grades without improving your skills, you will almost surely be disappointed down the line—if not in college, in your career. If you need it, you should be getting criticism—constructive, but tough criticism—on your grasp of the facts and issues, your logic, and your writing. This is what everyone else will be getting. Encouragement is important, of course, but you shouldn't get an easy ride. You are in college to learn—so you can profit from the knowledge and critical judgment of people trained in special areas. Don't let yourself be short-changed, no matter how sincere the motives.

You should also be sure that the major you choose is one *you* really want. Certain stereotypes exist about what majors are most interesting to what minority groups (for instance, that Blacks don't like math while Chinese- and Japanese-Americans do); this may unconsciously be affecting your adviser's guidance. Tradition alone is no reason to become an engineer or a social worker.

What Not to Do

Many special admissions programs have a social as well as an academic center. Don't get too involved in this social center or in any social or extracurricular group, whether it is the Black Student Union, the school

paper, campus politics, or whatever. School work should come first with all students, *especially* for special admissions students in their first year. Be sure you don't sign up for an overload (see Chapter 8). You won't save time or money if you end up repeating courses because you failed.

A date, a movie, or a party a week is the most time off you should give yourself until your grades are in good shape. A party should not be one that lasts until 3 a.m. and includes a half keg of beer and a half quart of Southern Comfort. You want to take Saturday night off, not all day Sunday too.

Similarly, you should not go home every weekend unless it is *absolutely* necessary, no matter how much you miss your family and friends. You need the library and a quiet place to study; you probably won't find either at home. In addition, if you go home all the time you will never find out what there is to do on campus and will miss out on that part of your education.

What if There Is No Special Admissions Program?

You may still be a special admissions student. To make a student feel better or to protect a school's reputation, some colleges do not tell people they are special admissions students. We frankly don't think much of this policy. It doesn't help the student who is struggling hard in class and doesn't know why s/he is having so much trouble. Be realistic. Talk to other students about what courses they took in high school. Visit your adviser. If you keep at it, you will finally get the information you need. You'll usually find courses on reading or study skills, open to everyone, where you'll meet other students with problems like yours. Knowing you are not alone can be a big help.

Even if a school doesn't say you are a special admissions student, it is up to you to realize you are not prepared and to do something about it. Don't give up, don't blame yourself, and don't blame all your problems on discrimination. Too much thinking about the past takes your mind off what you can do now. The college would not have admitted you if they didn't think there was a good chance you could do the job.

Foreign Students

Foreign students have many problems, the worst of which may be expecting few or no problems when they arrive. Most foreign students have done well in their home countries and have no real idea how bad it can be to cope with a new language and culture and school work in a foreign language all at the same time. You may be at more of a disadvantage than the American minority student whose second language is English; at least the American student knows the culture. Unless you have lived in the United States before, you probably don't.

Think About Your Program Carefully

Sign up for a light program your first year. Choose subjects that are familiar to you, so you will have a better chance of understanding the lectures. Many foreign students sign up for an overload (see Chapter 8) and then drop the courses by simply not showing up. This leads to F's, because it's against the rules to drop a course this way. Avoid the problem by taking a light load at first. You can go to summer school or carry a heavier load during the regular term once you are used to the United States.

Language Skills

Another reason to carry a light load at first is that your reading speed is much slower than it would be in your native language. It may have been cut by two-thirds. Even if you passed the Test of English as a Foreign Language (TOEFL), at first you may read English at the rate and level of a nine- or ten-year-old. Speak to your instructors ahead of time about possibly having a little more time to take exams or write papers because of your slow reading speed. Finally, don't take music courses unless you already know musical notation. This is like learning a third language!

Talk to Americans. Speak English constantly. Living in an international dorm with people from your own country can be relaxing, but if you wind up speaking your native language more than at a Saturday night party, you are hurting yourself. The best way to learn English is to speak it.

Transfer Credits

These are a major problem for foreign students. Delays in evaluation may cost you over a year's credit. You may not have gotten the college catalog in time or even at all, making it hard to see what you've already had and what you need. It is hard to have your credits evaluated in advance by mail but try to do so. As a backup, bring with you as much information as possible about your overseas college courses—texts, outlines, papers, etc. Unlike other transfer students, you won't be able to run home to get the information. Never give the college your only copy of the information about your courses. Always keep the original yourself.

Cultural Differences

Try to read everything you can about differences between your culture and the part of the United States where you are living. Things are done differently in different parts of the United States. Your embassy may have pamphlets. Talk to others from your country and ask at the campus foreign students office. If you can find a book about your culture by an American anthropologist (or one about America by someone from your country), read it. Many of the points may be relevant to differences in the two cultures.

All of us are raised with the idea that there is only one right way to do many small things, from being just late enough to a dinner party (2 minutes, 10 minutes, 20 minutes, an hour) to going to the bathroom (standing, sitting, squatting, left-handed or right-handed, with or without toilet paper, etc.) from bathing (twice a day, twice a week, twice a month, feet and face only, in showers or tubs) to which clothes are not modest (long pants, short dress, tight shirt, loose pants). It's hard to believe other people may find our culture's habits to be disgusting or compulsive or weird and their own bizzare behavior normal. The sooner you find out about these differences, the sooner you will be comfortable in the United States.

Social Problems

Two other major points of misunderstanding arise so often they are worth mentioning to all in-coming foreign students. The first may sound unimportant, but it may have a big effect on your social life—*social distance.* People in different countries stand at different distances when they talk. Americans stand fairly far apart compared to much of the world, and they are quite uncomfortable when people who are face-to-face with them move closer than an arm's length. If you move closer, it may seem to Americans to be romantic, sexual, or threatening. People who stand too close are also seen as "spraying germs all over my face." If Americans keep backing away from you as you talk, back off. On the other hand, Americans may think people who stand further apart than they do are cold and "stand-offish." It is hard to change the distance you have grown up with, but if you do, your social interactions will be much more successful.

The second point has to do with friends of the opposite sex. There is probably no part of your life in which you receive and send so many messages you are not aware of. Despair and heartbreak can be caused by the different ways in which foreign students and Americans see the same action or words. Your safest move is probably to avoid romance for a while — at least until you have a good American friend with whom you can talk things over. And when you do (or think you do) find romance, take it slowly — what is a proposal of marriage in one country may be a proposition for sexual relations in another and simple friendliness somewhere else. Your compliment may be an unintended insult — don't assume anything.

Money

Money is another constant problem for foreign students. Rules in your own country about how much money you may take out, changes in governments affecting your finances, U.S. willingness to accept your money, your lack of eligibility for many American loans, etc., complicate things if you need money right away. It is hard to plan to have extra money for emergencies, but if you can arrange to have some legal extra emergency money, do so. If not, be sure you have good contacts with your foreign students office. If you cannot raise tuition money, you may lose your student visa status. Arrangements made in advance can prevent this.

Veterans and Veterans' Dependents

Most colleges maintain some type of office to handle business related to veterans and dependents of veterans. Some offices provide counseling and tutoring; others deal strictly with financial matters and are located in the Bursar's (see page 31 in Chapter 3) or financial aid offices. For most veterans today, the problems are mainly financial or else similar to those of any older returning student.

Money

You may qualify for veterans' benefits if you are a veteran yourself, the dependent of a veteran who died, or a dependent of one who has a 100% disability rating (see your local veterans' office to find out). If you go to school full time, some of your living and school costs may be paid for, but there may be other financial benefits as well. For example, you may be allowed to postpone payments longer, even at the bookstore, or have all or part of the cost of a tutor covered. If you are a disabled veteran, there may be other benefits as well.

On the negative side, if you drop out in mid-term you may have to pay for the current term's courses yourself. This is especially likely to happen if you *didn't* get a tutor or otherwise show you were trying. It may also be harder for you to get scholarships if people think of you as taken care of by the Veterans Administration.

Academic Problems

Veterans generally have no unusual academic problems. One counselor we consulted mentioned that veterans tend to take mostly physical science courses. While this is not a problem in itself, if this applies to you remember that even the best engineer needs to write reports. If you ever plan to move into the higher levels of a company, you will find courses in the humanities, especially English, very worthwhile. It is also to your advantage as a person to know something outside your field. Don't make yourself too narrow. Because many veterans are working people with families, you may find the sections on commuting (pages 131-136 in Chapter 9) and returning students (pages 162-166 in this chapter) useful.

Handicapped Students

If there is one piece of advice the student with a physical handicap should take to heart, it is *never* leave anything to the last minute. There are times when you will have to fight for your rights and times when you'll have to put your pride in your pocket, but there will be a lot less of both if you are organized, plan ahead, and know the lay of the land.

Adjustments—By You and the College

Partly because of federal pressure and partly because of a desire to open educational opportunities to all qualified students, schools are making more efforts to adjust to handicapped students. You should not expect this adjustment to be complete yet because of the many different kinds of handicaps and the cost of being prepared for each. You may find braille elevator markings on one building and not in others, ramps into buildings with narrow bathroom doors, special elevators needing keys that are only available in offices you can't get to, etc. Despite the occasional fire alarm for the deaf, housing and parking generally are not good, and catalogs still use small print. Small schools usually do not have much money for physical changes, and large state schools are often caught up in red tape and bureaucracy.

The best way to deal with physical barriers is to plan ahead, beginning with a tour of the campus before you even register. If necessary, ask for an aide. While it will help in the future to agitate and work for changes,

remember that *you* have only a limited amount of energy, and the most important thing is to do well in your schoolwork. To deal with things as they are now, never register for a class without noticing where it is and figuring out how you will get there.

On the bright side, people — students and professors — are usually willing to be helpful if they know you need assistance and they know what to do. You must tell them. Look at it as an education for them, or simple politeness on your part. Habits are hard to break, but if your professor does not know you are lipreading, s/he can't even try to take your problem into account. You will need to tell him or her exactly what the problem areas are — s/he won't be able to guess; people without your particular handicap will not be able to figure out the implications on their own. If you can't mark your own exam, you must arrange with the professor *beforehand* to have someone help. Don't just turn up with your own helper the day of the exam. Also, by asking, you may be able to register separately and avoid the confusion and hours of waiting in line.

Tell people what you need, or they will assume you don't need anything. Being Superperson in a wheelchair and toughing it out or being too shy to speak up are both approaches that can get you on probation. One nice thing about college is that the people you find there are generally more interested in your brains than in anything else about you. Your handicap becomes a sort of technical difficulty. Unfortunately, faculty are much less informed than you about how to overcome these difficulties; so pass the word — for your own good and for those who come after you.

Take advantage of what the school does have. The library is likely to have, or be able to get, talking books, braillers, machines to blow up type, etc. The gym may offer special classes. Special parking stickers and spaces are usually available. There may be a handicapped students' office or a handbook, often written by other handicapped students. Talk to other students with your problems and find out how they managed. If they are still in school, they must be doing something right.

Don't let people steer you into traditional professional jobs for the handicapped if that isn't your interest. You shouldn't all wind up counseling handicapped children for a career. There is a tendency for advisers to steer you toward social science and education and away from natural sciences. Get an adviser in a field that interests *you* and stick to it and to him or her. Be both realistic and hard-nosed. A visual impairment may rule out neurosurgery as a career but not mathematics. The fact that lab benches are designed for standing people does not eliminate a premed major for someone in a wheelchair. Do what you want to do with your life, not necessarily what is easiest for the system.

Money

There are many sources of financial aid especially for handicapped students. You should check with your campus financial aid office and handicapped students' office for details. Agencies at both the state and federal level may provide funds, depending on your handicap (e.g., state commission for the visually handicapped, offices of vocational rehabilitation) and when and how it came to be (e.g., Veterans Administration, Social Security Disability benefits). Presumably you know quite a bit about local funds already, but by becoming a student you now become eligible for new categories—check and see. The catch is that you usually have to register as a full-time student. Fortunately, in many schools "full time" is defined as slightly less than a normal course load, so even if you have decided to carry a light load your first term, you may still be eligible.

Returning Students

A returning student is one who has been out of school for a number of years, on the average 10 or more, and is now beginning school again. S/he may have been working or raising a family and been out of school much longer than the stopping out student (see Chapter 8)—long enough for high school or early college skills to become rusty. Shaky study skills and being uneasy about them are among the biggest problems of the returning student. Worry about their families runs a close second.

Many returning students did well in high school or early college but are now afraid that the Biology 1 they had 20 years ago is out of date, to say nothing of forgotten. They are worried that they have completely forgotten how to study, and that they will do badly in classes with 18-year-olds who are right out of high school. There is some truth to all these worries, but fortunately there is a fairly simple way out.

Getting Back Into Things

If your main worry is that you no longer remember how to study, start slowly. Take one course at first; the next term take two. You can always make up for a slow start in summer school if time is important, but it is *more* important not to get in over your head and get discouraged your first term. Starting with one or two B's gives you (and your family) a lot more pep than starting with three D's. Your study skills will come back, but it takes time (like riding a bicycle but more slowly!). It might help to know that most returning students do quite well in the end. Perhaps this is partly because they have the advantage over many 18-year-olds of really wanting to be in school and knowing why they are there. Meanwhile, read Chapters 4 and 5 on study skills. This is especially important if you weren't a particularly good student before.

Out-of-Date Courses

Some fields change faster than others. A six-year-old course on genetics may be quite out of date, but a 16-year-old composition course may not. You usually have the choice of repeating out-of-date courses (although you won't usually get credit for a course you repeat). Whether or not you take a course again depends on a lot of things. These include whether or not your major department demands or allows it, how important the course is to your major or your plans (taking an updated genetics course may be more

important to a premed major than to a fine arts major), and how important the course is to you personally (you may feel that you want to know
modern genetics, no matter what your major is). If the choice is up to you,
you may prefer to buy an up-to-date textbook and brush up on the topic by
yourself. Remember, though, that very few people have the self-discipline
to learn a field as well by themselves as they would under the deadlines and
rules of a class.

A second problem with courses taken a long time ago is that you may
not have enough information about them to allow your new school to
evaluate them. Dig out your old college catalog, papers you wrote,
notebooks, exams, anything you can find. If you threw out everything,
write to your old school (or visit if it's nearby) and ask them to photocopy
the relevant pages of the catalog from your year; somewhere the college
must have a collection of its old catalogs. The department that gave the
course may even have a file of old course syllabi.

Family Problems

Your family problems will be different if you are usually the breadwinner, in charge of childcare and home, or both. Although people tend
to think of returning students as housewives, in fact in many schools the
returning student is now almost as likely to be male as female.

The Returning Homemaker

If you are a returning homemaker, it is particularly wise to begin with
just one or two courses. This is not only good for the academic reasons we
mentioned above, but because it gives your family time to get used to your
being a student. While family support is usually high for returning
students (maybe because they don't return unless it is), many people in
your family may not have thought through what it means to them if you
have exams or term papers to complete. On the basis of students' experiences we especially recommend going slowly while you have preschool
children.

At first, it may seem that you can easily handle two or three classes while
your children are in nursery school three mornings a week. But don't forget
parking time, library time, peace-and-quiet study time (while you're still
wide-awake enough to study), to say nothing of all the illnesses
preschoolers catch when they first go out into the world. If your only free

time is late evenings and 9 to 11:30 three mornings a week, we strongly suggest one course as a starter. On the other hand, we do recommend that you start—putting it off will just make it seem more scary—and one course is really not too much.

You also might want to consider day-care. Many campuses now have a day-care center for the children of faculty, students, and staff. Other common sources of child care (other than relatives and trading off with neighbors) are campus babysitting coops, student employment offices, and ads in local papers for people who care for children either in your home or theirs. Check with the local women's center (even if you are a father in this situation) and/or returning students office for other suggestions.

The Breadwinner

If you are the breadwinner in your family we also advise starting with one or two courses to warm up. Many colleges offer some evening courses. Quitting your job to carry a full load, with the financial hardship that usually follows, would be even harder to take if you don't do well because your study skills are rusty. As the breadwinner you should look into the financial benefits of actually enrolling in a degree-granting program (being a **matriculated** student), rather than just taking courses. Part-time non-matriculated students may not be eligible for financial aid, while part-time matriculated students may be.

How to Deal With Problems in General

Whatever your family problems, it is best to discuss them before you take your first course and then again after you have tried it out and seen how it really works for you. As things change (you take more courses, your children get older) you will need to sit down together again. A planned discussion of your needs, their needs, and of new ways to help each other is what is called for.

Your Goals

Many returning students who have had little or no college prefer to start at a two-year community college and plan to transfer later. If you were not an outstanding high school student this is probably a good idea. Community college courses have flexible hours, don't cost much, are small, and have a lot of support services that larger institutions lack. You should, however, read our chapter on community colleges, remembering that if you hope to transfer there are certain definite things you should and shouldn't do. Remember also that it is often possible to transfer after one year or one term or one course, rather than staying the entire two years.

If you are returning to school with the hope of using your B.A. to help you find a job, choose your major carefully. In many fields a B.A. can help you get an entry-level job but no more. Your age may be held against you (despite the increasing number of laws against age discrimination), and you may not want these jobs since they usually only pay entry-level wages.

Spend time with your counselors. Choose a major that you like, but one that will meet your career goals as well. Some schools have a returning students' center. This can be a lot of help both in practical tips (e.g., how to find sitters) and for general moral support (how to work up the nerve to speak in class that first time). It's good to make friends with younger students, but it is good for morale to talk to people who know what you are going through, too. Among other things you'll find that you are not the only one who felt "old" at first, and that while you may notice it almost no one else does!

12.

The Student Body: You and Your Campus Health Service

Being sick is almost always terrible. You feel bad, you miss classes and tests, and your social life falls apart. To make matters worse, for those of you living away from home, your family and a familiar doctor are not there to help. It's usually up to you and your campus health service to deal with what's wrong with you. This chapter will give you some idea of what to expect, and what *not* to expect, from your campus health service. It will also offer some suggestions about what to keep in mind whenever you're sick, at school or elsewhere.

The usual student health service is staffed by local doctors working at the campus part-time. Students are seen on a walk-in basis—first come, first served—with a doctor on call for emergencies at night and on weekends. The number of doctors available and the services offered differ from campus to campus. Some handle only very basic health problems and send students to off-campus doctors for more specialized illnesses. Many larger health services, however, run specialty clinics themselves. These clinics, such as allergy, gynecology, and dermatology, see students by appointment only.

Is College Hazardous to Your Health?

Despite late hours studying or partying, dorm food, and the pressures of college life, college students are remarkably healthy. The most common problems seen at campus health services are the same ones found in people the same age who are not going to college. Heading the list of common illnesses seen on a walk-in basis are colds, flu, sore throats, and earaches. Bronchitis and pneumonia round out the list.

Perhaps you are surprised to see that the list looks so ordinary. In particular, you may have noted the absence of mononucleosis ("mono") from the list. Mononucleosis, as you probably know, is also known as the "kissing disease," because it can be caught that way. The main symptoms are a slight fever and continual lack of energy. Rumors could lead you to believe it is almost as common as a cold. The fact is, however, that mononucleosis is fairly unusual. The director of a health center at a campus with 17,000 students estimates that 30 to 40 cases are treated there each year—hardly an epidemic. Actually, if you feel tired a great deal of the time, the cause is much more likely to be lack of sleep, poor diet, or stress (see below) than mono.

Problems seen in specialty clinics are also unsurprising. Acne is the most common problem treated in the dermatology clinic, while backaches and sprains (often the result of sports injuries) are frequently seen at the orthopedic clinic.

One of the most widely used specialty clinics is gynecology. Gynecology clinics mainly provide routine pelvic examinations for women. Some also provide birth control services, pregnancy tests, and abortion counseling. Many young women feel awkward or embarrassed about going to the gynecologist, especially at a campus clinic. Sexual activity and related medical care are dealt with much more openly on most college campuses than they were even ten years ago, but you are the best judge of how comfortable you would feel about going to a campus clinic for these purposes. If you are concerned about confidentiality, don't hesitate to ask who, besides the doctor, might see your records (e.g., student clerks). Whatever you decide, the important thing is not to go without medical care when it is needed. Go off campus if you must.

Mind and Body—A Two-Way Street

The director of a large university health service estimates that over half the students seen at the health center in a given week have problems like headaches, digestive problems, or lack of energy. These symptoms do not seem to be caused by any particular disease. The problem of symptoms with no "cause" is not restricted to campus health services; doctors everywhere report it. What are these mystery illnesses?

At the present time, medical science believes they are caused by anxiety. The exact relationship between mind and body is one of the great unknowns in medicine, but there is a lot of evidence showing that the mind and body affect each other.

Many people are upset by the suggestion that their physical symptoms are "mental." They think either the doctor doesn't believe the symptoms are real, or that the doctor is calling them unstable or crazy. Neither of these is necessarily true. Doctors know that where symptoms come from has nothing to do with how real they are. They also know that anxiety is a common and severe problem. When anxiety grows to the point where it is hurting your health, it helps to have someone point it out and suggest ways of dealing with it.

Sometimes just being made aware of the problem is enough to solve it. Students can often take the necessary steps themselves to deal with school or personal pressures. You may, though, need outside help. Fortunately, most student health services can provide that help through a counseling center. Often all that is needed is a visit or two with an experienced counselor, but sometimes more therapy is needed to get at the problem.

Don't hesitate to go to the counseling or psychological centers on your campus if you need them. College can be an intense, stressful experience, and getting help in coping can be the wisest thing you do (see Chapter 8).

"But Can't They See How Sick I Am? How Can I Be Asked to Wait?"

The most frequently heard complaint about student health services is the time spent waiting to see a doctor. During periods of highest demand, waits as long as an hour or two are common. The problem, as you might expect, is financial. Health services cost a lot to run (if they are to remain free to the students), and most universities cannot afford enough doctors so that you can walk in and see one at once. Emergencies, of course, are the exception.

Is there anything you can do to shorten the time spent in the health service waiting room? We have two suggestions. Go at a time when the health service is least busy—generally from around 10:00 to 3:00 Tuesday through Thursday. The worst times are Monday mornings and Friday afternoons. A second step you can take is to learn when they can help you and when they can't. Many of the problems seen at the health service are those for which modern medicine has no cure. Time and your own body usually cure them.

Everyone's time could be saved if students spotted these problems and did some simple things for themselves. For example, science does not yet have a cure for the common cold, and your doctor can do little beyond providing a note if you miss an exam and recommending rest, fluids, and an occasional aspirin if you have a headache. If this sounds surprisingly like what your grandmother recommended for a cold, it does because it is! In fact, grandmothers have been way ahead of medical science in this area. A recent study has shown that chicken soup actually does help get rid of cold symptoms. We don't mean to suggest that home cures are the answer to all your medical problems, but we do feel that it's important to be able to tell which problems need professional care and which do not.

"But No One Seems to Care!"

After what may be a long wait to see a doctor, a health service exam often seems short and not very thorough. The doctor is usually a stranger. Too often the student may come away with a prescription for little pink pills and the feeling that the doctor doesn't really care.

Some of us over 30 remember when the old family doctor would come to our bedside any hour of the day or night to take care of us. In some cases, the doctor became a close family friend. Even those of us who never knew such a doctor in real life found one in Marcus Welby, M.D., of TV fame. The show was immensely popular because Welby was everything a doctor should be—wise, warm, caring, knowledgeable, and there when you needed him.

Clinics just cannot meet all these expectations. The personal relationship between doctor and patient, time to talk, and how long you have to wait are the three things that suffer most. If you think about it, though, these are not really the most important parts of good health care.

Most health services will allow you to see a particular doctor if you ask. If you find a doctor you like, you may be able to see the same one each time. You may have to wait a bit longer, and the doctor you want to see may not be working on the day you want to see him or her, but it is worth asking. Don't feel hurt, though, if the doctor doesn't recognize you. The average health service physician sees a lot of patients in an eight-hour day!

Be ready to describe your symptoms clearly. How long have you felt tired? Have you had a fever—if so, how high was it? What did you eat the day before you broke out in hives? A good description of your symptoms can help the doctor figure out what you've got.

Do not insist on medicine if the doctor doesn't prescribe any. Some patients feel they have not been treated if they don't get medication. This feeling can sometimes encourage a doctor to prescribe drugs that may *at best* do no harm (but certainly not help). Antibiotics, for example, do nothing to cure illness caused by a virus (such as the common cold).

If medicine *is* prescribed for you, *ask* what it is. Be sure to find out about any side effects, including those that might be caused by taking it along with other medicines or alcohol. If you have any questions about your illness or the treatment prescribed, ask. It is a very rare doctor who will not provide this kind of information when asked.

"It Sounds as if I Almost Have to Be a Doctor Myself!"

Good health care has two important parts—the provider of health care service (usually a doctor or nurse) and you. Surprisingly, many people know even less about how their bodies work than they do about how their cars work. They turn their bodies over to a doctor when it doesn't work in the same way they leave their cars for repair. Few people actually stop to think of it in this way, but it is, unfortunately, an accurate analogy.

If you want to learn more about your body, a college-level biology course is a fine place to start. Articles on medical topics in good, popular magazines are a source of general information; so are newspaper stories. Even medical journals can be useful if you want to get the most up-to-date information on a particular topic. The most difficult sounding article can often be read by someone with a basic background and a medical dictionary nearby. Medical journals and dictionaries can be found in large public libraries or campus medical school libraries, which are usually open to all students.

Knowing more can be useful in several ways. You will be in a better position to give the doctor information and to understand what s/he says, and you will be better prepared to ask and decide about different treatments. And, as a bonus, you may learn how to take better care of yourself, so you won't have to see a doctor as often. We've listed some books that may be helpful.

Suggested Readings

Boston Women's Health Collective. *Our Bodies, Ourselves: A Book By and For Women.* New York: Simon & Schuster, Inc., 1979.

Royal Canadian Air Force. Exercise Plans for Physical Fitness. 1976.

Shapiro, H. J. *The Birth Control Book: A Complete Guide for Men and Women.* New York: Avon Books, 1978.

The Diagram Group. *Man's Body: An Owner's Manual.* New York: Paddington Press, Ltd., 1979.

Vickery, D. M., and Fries, J. F. *Take Care of Yourself: A Consumer's Guide to Medical Care.* Reading, MA: Addison-Wesley Publishing Co., 1976.

13.

Looking Ahead — Planning for the Future

If you've read this far, you probably have a pretty good idea of what college is all about and how best to deal with the day-to-day kinds of problems you'll run into. In this chapter, we'll talk about how to use your college experience to plan for the future, especially for further schooling or a job. After all, a college graduation ceremony is called "commencement," which means "beginning" rather than "ending."

What Should I Major In?

Two of the most important decisions you'll make concerning college are selecting which college to attend in the first place and choosing a major. While neither is irreversible — you can switch colleges and majors — it's best to make these decisions as carefully as you can the first time.

We briefly discussed majors in Chapter 2 under the topic "Planning Your Program." A major is a field of study, like chemistry or English, that you concentrate on. Faculty in each area set up guidelines that students majoring in the field must follow. It is usually necessary to know a field very well in order to decide what is really important to that area. This is why faculty decide on the requirements, rather than leaving it entirely up to the students. Choosing a major depends on what you enjoy studying and are good at and on what you plan to do when you graduate.

I Want to be a " _____ . "

In some cases, choosing a major is easy. If you want to be an electrical engineer, a major in electrical engineering is the obvious choice. A major in English would be a good choice for someone wanting to teach English in high school. In other situations, the choice is not so easy. Suppose you plan to go to law school after graduation. What is the best major? It might surprise you to learn that most law schools are eager to accept highly qualified applicants regardless of their majors. Law is a field that cuts across so many other areas that law school admissions people feel good work in almost any major is a sign you'll do well in law school. Medical schools have the same philosophy. They usually have specific course requirements (e.g., organic chemistry, general biology), but it is possible to fulfill these and still be, for example, an art or math major. If you know what kind of career you want, it is well worth the time to find out what courses employers or graduate school admissions committees will look for. Your adviser, the campus career office, the preprofessional advising office, and the library are good places to start looking for information. You may find you have much more freedom in the courses you can choose than you thought.

Also, remember you'll have a chance to take a number of courses outside your major. These classes should be chosen as carefully as those in your major. They represent a chance to explore a subject you've always been interested in or an opportunity to give yourself an extra edge in the job market because of a special combination of skills. For example, someone interested in a career in business might decide to learn two foreign languages in order to be ready for jobs that require international travel.

"I'm Not Sure What I Want to Do"

But what if you don't have a specific career goal? Despite the fact that it seems that everyone (everyone but you, that is!) knows exactly what they want to do after they finish college, a large number of students do *not* have specific plans. Many intend to look for a job and feel a college degree will be helpful, but they don't have a particular type of job in mind.

Students in this category have the most freedom of all choosing courses and a major. Our basic advice is to choose a major based on your interests and aptitudes, while making sure you get a good background in basic skills like writing and math.

The Graduate School Option

Over half of all incoming freshmen plan to go on for some form of schooling after college. Some students will take time off after graduation to work for a while before returning to school full time, while others plan to go straight through. Still others will take advantage of an increasing number of part-time programs that allow them to work full time and take courses in the late afternoon or evening.

Is graduate school for you? It all depends on the kind of career you are interested in. For some fields, on-the-job experience is the best preparation. Getting a good job after college that gives you this experience is often the best thing you can do. For other fields, formal graduate training is essential. A person who wants to be a veterinarian, for example, must complete a four-year program, including courses and clinical work with patients, after finishing college.

The career office on your campus is a good place for information about different careers and what, if any, graduate training they require. You may find out that there is more than one way to achieve the career goal you have in mind. If you are interested in law, for example, a much shorter program can train you to be a legal assistant or paralegal. The career office should be able to give you the information you need about different options.

Kinds of Graduate Programs

Although they are usually referred to as "graduate school," there are really three different kinds of programs you can take after graduating from college. One category is referred to as "professional school." These programs prepare you to enter a specific profession such as medicine (M.D. degree), dentistry (D.D.S. degree), law (J.D. degree), or business (M.B.A. degree).

A second category of programs is referred to simply as "graduate school." These programs, leading to a masters degree (Master of Arts [M.A.] or Master of Science [M.S.]) or doctoral degree (Doctor of Philosophy [Ph.D.]), are usually offered in traditional academic fields such as English, chemistry, or sociology. Graduate programs prepare people in a specific area but usually not for a specific job.

If you are in a four-year college, most of your professors probably have a Ph.D. degree. Few, if any, of their courses dealt with college teaching per se. The idea is that the most important part of graduate training is acquiring basic knowledge in a field and learning how to do research in that area. In most master's programs you take courses for one or two years and complete a research project (a Master's Thesis); some programs, though, require only courses. For a Ph.D. program you usually take courses for two to three years and do a larger research project (a Ph.D. thesis or dissertation). These programs may take from three to five years, and sometimes more. In some fields, you may also do some practical, applied work; for example, for a Ph.D. in clinical psychology you might take courses, do a thesis, and complete some clinical work with people with problems.

A third type of graduate program involves technical training. Programs to prepare people to be medical technologists, for example, fall into this category, as do paralegal training courses. These programs are usually shorter than the others and can take one year or less.

In the section that follows, we'll talk about some of the things you'll need to know before you begin applying to graduate school (we'll use the term "graduate school" to refer to all three categories of programs, except when we say otherwise). In fact, it's never too early to become familiar with this information because it may help you make better choices during college — before you're actually ready to think about applying to graduate school.

Not everything we say will apply equally to all kinds of programs. That is why it is so important to see an adviser early to get the specific information you'll need for the program(s) you are most interested in.

How to Select a School

In thinking about where to apply to graduate school, you should consider the quality of the department, as well as the reputation of the university as a whole. Many fine institutions have several weak departments, while many less prestigious schools have some excellent ones.

Reputation and Program

The reputation of the faculty is the major factor in determining the quality of a department. Professors in the same field at your undergraduate college can help you with this. You may also want to go to the library to look up some of the research done by faculty at particular institutions to get some idea of their interests. This is especially important if you are interested in a graduate program that will involve research as a major part of your training.

Other things to consider are the program and the facilities in a particular department. What is the department's orientation? Does it offer courses in the areas you wish to concentrate in? For example, you might think graduate study in anthropology is pretty much the same anywhere, but some departments may emphasize cultural and some physical anthropology. Another thing to think about is the style of education. Are students required to take a large number of courses or is emphasis placed on tutorial learning and participation in research? Are there adequate library and laboratory facilities?

Size is another consideration. Very large programs may mean crowded classes, less individual attention, and an impersonal feeling. Very small programs, on the other hand, may mean a shortage of excellent fellow students and a limited number of course offerings. It is important for you to know as much as you can about a program, so you can make the best choice for you.

You and Your Limitations

In selecting a school you must also think about your own record. Students usually find it very helpful to talk with faculty members and advisers at their own school to get a feel for programs they would have a good chance of being admitted to. Be sure to take a copy of your transcript with you when you talk to these people so they can help you realistically evaluate your options.

Finally, you should take geographic and financial considerations into account. If for personal or other reasons you are limited to a certain geographical area, be sure to tell your adviser this at the outset. It's also important for you to think about how you will pay for your graduate work. You need to find out about financial aid and how readily available it is at different schools (see page 189 later in this chapter). If you plan to go to school part time, it's important for you to know whether the school you are interested in allows part-time students.

Much of the information we've listed above can be found in graduate school catalogs; a collection of these catalogs can usually be found in your college's career center and in the library. Read the catalogs of the schools that interest you. You should then have enough information to decide if you want to find out more about certain schools.

How Hard Will It Be to Get In?

We're sure it comes as no surprise to you that competition for admission to certain programs is much greater than it is for others. At the present time, medical schools receive many more applications from qualified people than they can accept. Law programs are in a similar situation. Within any particular field, though, some schools are harder to get into than others. Competition may be rough even if there aren't many people competing. For example, few students may be applying for graduate study in French literature, but a handful of universities with the most prestigious programs may have many more applications than they have openings for new students.

Programs of any type with the best reputations get many more applications than they can accept. These programs can then be highly selective, while less popular programs leading to the same degree will be easier to get into. Advisers can generally give you some idea of how your record would compare with the other applicants to particular schools.

In some fields, such as medicine and psychology, books are available that give statistics on the average grades and standardized test scores of successful applicants at different universities. Of course, there is no guarantee you will be admitted if your scores are higher, nor do these data tell you you don't have a chance if your scores are lower. This information simply gives you some idea of how selective a school has been in the past.

How to Apply

The first step in the application process is to write directly to the departments you are interested in for information about their programs, financial aid opportunities, application forms, and most recent graduate catalog. You can do this with a postcard addressed to Graduate Admissions, Department of _____. Once you have this material, you can decide which programs you actually want to apply to.

Completing application forms can be a tedious, time consuming, and expensive process. Most schools charge a nonrefundable application fee of about $20; however, in cases of financial need the application fee is sometimes waived. In general (and there can be many exceptions), three to seven applications should be more than enough if you have carefully selected the schools. It is usually a good strategy to apply to one or two "safe" schools that you feel pretty sure of getting into, as well as to one that seems like wishful thinking. The rest should be schools you have a good chance for. This way, you may be pleasantly surprised and get into your number one choice, but in any case you have "covered" yourself.

Watch for Deadlines

It is important to meet application deadlines. These vary depending on the school and the kind of program. As you'll see below, an application consists of many parts, all of which must reach the school before a decision can be made. By starting to get your forms together well in advance of the deadlines, you'll be sure that your application will be carefully considered. Even if your late application *is* considered, you may have missed a chance to get financial support from a school.

It is also important to remember that you'll probably be involved in the application process at the same time you're taking a regular load of courses. Applying to graduate school does take time, and by starting early you'll be able to spread out the workload so it won't be too heavy at any one point.

What Goes Into an Application?

Graduate school is an investment, both for you and the school you will be attending. Depending on the type of program, you may be a graduate student anywhere from less than a year to four or more. It's important to you and to the faculty members who will be your teachers that there be a good match between your interests and abilities and what the program requires. What do graduate school admission committees look for when reviewing applications?

Grades

Your grades are probably the most essential factor in determining whether you will be admitted to a highly competitive program. The better your grades, the better your chances of getting into the school you want. They are certainly not the only factor, as you'll see later on, but they are important. Graduate school admission committees also look at transcripts to see what kind of courses you took and whether there was any trend in your grades (up or down) over the years you were in college.

Some students become so concerned about grades that they take only easy courses to be sure they will graduate with a high grade point average. Graduate school admissions committees know that some classes are more difficult than others, and they take this into account when evaluating your record. If a student has avoided challenging courses, it will be clear from the record. Committees also know that it takes some students as long as a year or two to "find themselves" in college, and that grades early on in your college career may not give an accurate picture of your true potential.

Recommendations

Most graduate programs ask for three letters of reference from people who are in a position to judge your ability. Letters of reference are often a problem for students. They find themselves in their senior year of college with a handful of forms to be filled out by faculty members who know them. The forms ask about academic promise, motivation, maturity, etc., and many students find they can't think of a single faculty member who would remember them.

Graduate schools realize that large classes often make it impossible for students to get to know a number of faculty members really well. They do expect, though, that the best applicants will have taken one or more small seminars (see Chapter 5) or will have excelled in a large class, so that at least one or two faculty members will be able to write more than "Jane Doe took my course and got a B." As we've said earlier, it's a good idea to get to know faculty, both to enrich your education and to be able to get meaningful letters of reference.

In thinking about whom to ask to write these letters for you, remember that a strong letter from an assistant professor who is not yet well-known is much better than a mediocre one from a famous professor. Of course, a strong letter from a famous professor is best of all! In any case, it is important that the person be able to say something meaningful about your potential for graduate study.

Many students are reluctant to approach faculty to ask them for a recommendation. There is no reason to feel awkward about this; professors are often asked to write letters of recommendation, and they are generally happy to help students in this way. Remember, though, to observe certain rules of etiquette when making your request. Don't just leave a note in the professor's mailbox asking him or her to write a letter for you. Be sure to see the professor first during office hours to briefly discuss your plans and your record. It's a good idea to bring along a copy of your transcript, a written description of your career goals, and your application essay (discussed later in this chapter) to leave with the professor. It also helps remind the professor about your work if you leave a copy of your term paper or a good exam.

Don't hesitate to ask the professor if s/he can write a strong letter for you. Professors will generally tell you when they don't feel they will be able to do so. In this case, thank the professor for his or her time and seek out another reference.

Do all this well in advance of application deadlines. It is bad form (and can lead to bad results) to ask for letters just a few days before they are due. Give your references at least a month, preferably more, to prepare your letter. Evaluative letters of this sort are difficult to write, and a rush job is usually not to the student's advantage. If your request is last minute, the letter may not even get out in time to be part of your file at all.

Many colleges have a service that allows professors to fill out a single, standardized recommendation form that is then sent to the list of schools provided by the student. This saves faculty a great deal of time. Most graduate school admission committees do not mind if the recommendation they receive is a photocopy and not on their "official" form. If your college has such a service, use it; remember that you are not the only student asking professors for recommendations. Anything you can do to make the job easier for them will be greatly appreciated and help get your files completed by the deadline.

As a final note, you may be aware of recent laws that allow students to see certain educational records and files. Most recommendation forms ask the student to indicate whether s/he waives the right to see it. Many professors prefer not to or are unwilling to write recommendations unless this right has been waived, even though the letter may be very supportive. They feel that a system in which letters are confidential is more honest. If you have done well in a course and asked the professor directly if s/he would be able to support your application, you can probably feel comfortable not actually seeing the letter.

Test Scores

Many graduate schools require all applicants to take one or more standardized tests and to arrange for their scores to be sent directly to the schools. There is a lot of controversy about the usefulness of these tests in predicting success in graduate school, but most programs feel they are the only means a graduate school has to compare students, using exactly the same standard in each case.

Find out well in advance what standardized tests are required by the schools you'll be applying to. Medical schools, for example, require the Medical College Admission Test (MCAT), usually taken in the spring before your senior year. Most professional schools (e.g., medicine, law, dentistry, management, etc.) have their own tests. Be sure to check with an adviser on your campus to learn which test(s) to take and when.

Most graduate schools (as distinct from the professional schools mentioned above) ask students to take the Graduate Record Examination (GRE). The GRE has two parts. The Aptitude Test is a three-hour test of general scholastic ability appropriate for the graduate level. The questions check your ability to understand, analyze, and interpret materials, as well as your interpretation of numerical data, reasoning, and problem solving. The Advanced Test, also three hours, measures your mastery in a specific field such as math or history. Some schools require the Aptitude Test only, while others ask applicants to take the Advanced Test as well.

It is important for you to find out *when* you will have to take these tests so that your scores will be available by your application deadline. The career office at your college should have test brochures that will give you a description of the test, as well as some sample questions and answers. These pamphlets also include the form you will have to fill out in advance to arrange to take the test.

Should You Try to Prepare for These Tests?

Can you raise your scores significantly by studying for standardized tests? Studying might help with tests dealing with specific subject matter such as the GRE Advanced Tests or the basic science part of the MCAT. If it has been a long time since you've used your high school algebra or geometry or you are just generally weak in math, get out your books and brush up on the basics for the math part of the General Aptitude Test. It's probably harder to prepare for tests of vocabulary, comprehension, and reasoning because these abilities build up after many years of education and don't lend themselves easily to cramming.

We do feel, though, that it helps for students to be as familiar as possible with the kinds of questions they will be asked. You can do this without an expensive coaching course. Six or seven dollars spent on one of the many sample test books that gives both questions and answers may be a wiser investment than two or three hundred dollars for a coaching course.

Finally, remember that test scores are just one part of your application, and admissions committees are well aware that a three-hour test may not adequately reflect a person's true ability. If you have an especially bad day when you take one of these tests, you might want to consider retaking it on the next test date. This way, schools will have both sets of scores and will be likely to place more weight on the higher one.

Personal Statements

Most applications ask students to send a statement about their background and plans for graduate work. Students frequently underestimate the importance of the statement. Often, it is the only thing that makes you stand out from a whole pile of otherwise equally qualified applicants.

Be honest in your statement, and above all make sure it is well-written. Have someone whose judgment you trust read it over critically. Faculty members and advisers are usually glad to do this. There are few things less impressive than an awkwardly written, grammatically incorrect, or pompous personal statement. On the other hand, one that is well-written and interesting is a real plus. Make sure that yours falls into this last category.

Your statement gives you an opportunity to tell the admissions committee about your background, highlighting anything you feel would be of interest to the committee and might strengthen your application. It gives you a chance to mention any research or relevant work experience you've had as well as your community service and involvement in student organizations. Professional schools, in particular, are interested in the extracurricular activities you've been involved in.

If you are applying to several schools (and especially if you are applying to more than one type of program) be sure your statement is appropriate for each application. You may have to modify it for each one. This takes time, but it is worth the effort.

Interviews

Most medical schools, and some other professional schools as well, require a personal interview as part of the application process. These schools first screen the applications they receive, selecting from these a group of individuals who are then invited to an interview. Schools usually hold regional interviews in different cities throughout the country, so you will probably not have to travel far.

What are these interviews like, and how can you prepare for them? First, remember that an interview is not an interrogation, but rather an opportunity for the interviewer(s) to find out more about you and your plans. The interviewer is not only interested in why you want to go into a specific field but also in the *way* in which you answer that question. Are you able to communicate well orally, and do you deliver your answers with confidence? Do you have the personal characteristics that the school would like to see in its students as well as in future professionals?

Be sure to do your homework before each interview. Read the catalog carefully and be prepared to ask one or two questions about the program when you are given an opportunity at the end of the interview. Asking intelligent questions shows that you are both smart and genuinely interested. Asking ones that are answered in the material you have been sent does not.

Appearance is important in interviews. Be sure to dress appropriately and neatly and pay particular attention to "personal grooming" (e.g., clean hair, fingernails, body, and breath; unwrinkled clothes; polished shoes). This not only helps create a favorable impression, but you will feel more confident as well. Another bit of advice we offer is to get a good night's sleep before the interview and *allow plenty of time to get to the interview.* The last thing you need to worry about is whether you'll make it there on time!

Don't be surprised if you come away from an interview feeling that you have no idea how it went. Some interviewers give no hints about how you are doing or how they feel about you either during the interview or afterward. Many students have been pleasantly surprised to be accepted by a school after what they were sure was a bad interview.

How Do I Pay for It All?

Many graduate students are able to get some form of financial aid to support themselves while studying. The availability of aid and the form it takes varies considerably depending on the kind of degree you are seeking. The major type of financial aid for medical students, for example, is loans. Students in Ph.D. programs, on the other hand, usually have a wider range of options.

Fellowships, which can range from a few hundred to several thousand dollars per year, are grants given to a student without any service expected in return. **Assistantships**, however, require the recipient to perform certain duties and are most common in Ph.D. programs. The service may vary from reading exam papers in a freshman class to actual classroom teaching to working on a research project. The assistantship can provide the recipient with valuable experience, in addition to money to support his or her education. Student loans from banks do not require any service, but they must eventually be repaid.

Be sure to request information about financial aid when you write to a school for application materials. Although most students receive their support directly from the school they attend or from banks, there are also many other awards through foundations and governmental agencies. The career office at your school should be able to give you information about these. These awards are usually highly competitive, but winning one can make your life easier financially and can serve as an honor as well.

But What if I Don't Get In?

The months between the time you send applications and the time you actually hear from schools can seem endless. The floor leading to many a mailbox has been well worn by students anxiously waiting for each day's delivery.

We hope that your own efforts to apply to graduate school have a happy ending. Most students who have had good guidance along the way are accepted by one or more of the schools they apply to. But what if you are not one of these? What if the net result of all your efforts is a collection of "we are sorry to inform you" letters?

The most important thing to remember is that a rejection from a school (or several schools) does not mean you are an unworthy or a second-rate person. Schools try to make the best match between their programs and students who wish to participate in these programs. By and large they do a good job of selecting, but the process is far from perfect. If you are not accepted, it is worth trying to understand why.

Some schools simply get many more applications from qualified people than they have places for. If after talking to an adviser you agree your record is a good one, consider reapplying again (possibly to some less competitive schools) next year.

Perhaps upon reexamination you find your record is not as strong as you thought. Is there anything you can do to improve it? Consider if additional specific undergraduate courses would help, or perhaps some relevant research experience. Reapplying at a later date might then be the best thing to do.

Yet another approach is to consider other careers in related fields. A person wanting to become an opthalmologist (a physician specializing in the surgical and nonsurgical treatment of eye diseases) might be equally happy as an optometrist (a specialist trained in the diagnosis and treatment of vision problems). The competition for admission to an optometry program is usually less than that to a medical school, and for this particular person the end results might be just as satisfactory. A large number of such alternatives exist, and they are not second-rate options. Your career office should be able to help you identify them.

As a final note, remember that even the most highly qualified people don't always win first prize. The story goes that when Charlie Chaplin entered a Charlie Chaplin look-alike contest, he came in third!

How to Plan a Career (and Land a Great Job)

Suppose you've decided that graduate school is not for you, or that you want to work for a while before going back to school. How do you go about getting yourself a job?

Statistics show that the average worker over 35 is involved in job hunting once every three years. For workers under 35, the figure is once every one-and-a-half years. In addition, the average person changes careers (and not just jobs) from three to five times in a lifetime. Clearly, it is to your advantage to learn as much as you can about how to look for a job, whether you're doing it for the first time as a new college graduate or for the tenth.

There are a number of excellent books available that discuss job hunting in great detail. We have listed some at the end of this chapter that we think are especially helpful. We strongly recommend that you look at one or more of these because we can't give you all the information you'll need in just a few pages. What we plan to do in this section is highlight what we feel are some of the most important key points in job hunting. The details can be readily found elsewhere.

Self-Assessment

Most experts agree that the first step in the job-seeking process is self-assessment. Self-assessment simply means knowing about yourself. You need to take a careful look at your previous experiences and accomplishments in order to identify what you enjoy doing and what your skills are. Ask yourself questions along the following lines:

- What are my skills?
- Do I want to work with people, data, or things?
- What does success mean to me?
- What kind of environment do I want?

The career office on your campus can help you do your self-assessment. You may also find it useful to write a description of your ideal job; this will probably answer many of the questions you need to ask yourself as you do your self-assessment.

The Working World

Once you have this basic information about yourself, you need to learn more about the kinds of careers and jobs that match your skills and interests. Here too the career office on your campus can be of help. Set up an appointment to talk with an adviser and take advantage of the career planning library that many of them have.

It's also an excellent idea to talk directly with people who are employed in the type of job you're thinking about. Just by telling friends and relatives about your plans, you may be able to identify people who can help you get information. Professional associations or trade unions for people in various career areas (e.g., realtors, interior decorators, electricians, etc.) can also be helpful in suggesting someone you can speak to. In talking with people, you'll want to ask such things as how they spend their working day, what they like and dislike about their jobs, and how best to go about getting a similar job. Most people are happy to share this kind of information with you. Just be sure to follow up each discussion with a brief thank-you note to ensure their willingness to help the person who comes after you and maybe to remember you kindly if they hear of a job.

Job Seeking

You've assessed your skills and have done your homework on the kinds of jobs that seem to best fit your needs and abilities. What next? Before you head out to find that great job, you need to take care of a few additional details, details that can make the difference between getting the job you want and missing out. These include writing a resume and cover and/or inquiry letters and learning how to handle an interview.

The Résumé

Your **résumé** is a summary of your experiences, skills, and objectives and is usually the basis for a potential employer's first impressions of you. It is important that your résumé present you in the best possible light, so that the employer will want to see the person behind it. There are many good books on job hunting that discuss different formats for a résumé. There is no one "right" or "perfect" format so we suggest you pick one that you like after looking at the various types. There are some general guidelines, however, that you should keep in mind regardless of the format you pick.

Length.   Keep your résumé brief. One page should be adequate for a new graduate.

Appearance.   An organized readable arrangement of information is important. If the résumé looks cluttered and hard to read, it may not be read at all. Errors of any sort—typographical, spelling, or grammatical— are unacceptable. If your résumé must be modified, retype it—do not make corrections by hand.

Content.   Include only the most relevant and important information about yourself. There is a natural tendency to put too much in—be sure to edit your résumé carefully. Emphasize special achievements and abilities. Never exaggerate or give false information. Since the résumé is likely to be scanned quickly at first, be sure it is concise and to the point.

A good book on job seeking will guide you on what categories of information should be included in your résumé and how much detail should be provided.

Letters to Employers

In the course of your job search, you will probably write several different kinds of letters to employers. An **inquiry letter** can help you find open positions or gain other useful information. It basically tells the employer what kind of job you are interested in and requests information about what you must do to be considered for a position.

A **cover letter** is one sent along with a copy of your résumé. It should tell the employer why you are contacting him or her, any special features of your record you want to bring to his or her attention, and what you want the employer to do.

Other kinds of letters you will probably be writing are (a) the **follow-up letter** to be sent a few days after an interview to show your interest in the job, (b) the **acknowledgement of job offer letter** that acknowledges receipt of a formal job offer without actually accepting it, (c) the **job rejection letter** to turn down a job offer, and (d) the **acceptance letter** (hooray!) to formally accept a job offer.

The most important letters are the cover and inquiry letters since these help determine whether you will be considered further for an opening. In all cases, though, letters should look good and be easy to read. They should be neat and free from any kind of error as well as organized and to the point. Your letters represent you, and you want to make the most favorable impression possible.

Interviews

The interview is often your first face-to-face contact with a potential employer. They will be trying to decide whether you will make a contribution to their company, and, at the same time, you are trying to decide whether a particular job is right for you.

Perhaps the best way to prepare for an interview is to ask yourself what you would be looking for in a prospective employee if you were the interviewer. Many of the questions you would probably have fall into two groups: one deals with why the company should hire that particular person and the other with why that person is interested in your particular company. As the interviewee, you should think about your answers to both questions: what do you have to offer this company, and why are you interested in them?

A few frequently asked job interview questions are shown in the box labeled "Interview Questions."

Interview Questions

- What are your long- and short-range career goals?

- Why did you choose _____ for a career?

- In what ways do you think you can make a contribution to our company?

- What was your most rewarding college experience?

- What three things are most important to you in a job?

- Why are you seeking a position with our company?

A good interviewer will ask open-ended questions that call for more than just a "yes" or "no" answer. Interviewers vary, however, in how well they do. Some will ask questions that let you present yourself in the best light, while others will waste time talking themselves or asking irrelevant questions. You may find yourself at times trying to rescue a bad interview by redirecting a question or otherwise shifting the discussion. Do this carefully, but by all means do it if necessary. The interview is your opportunity to show what you know and why the company should consider you. Be sure to make the most of that opportunity.

A few other points about job interviews are also worth noting. As we mentioned in our discussion of professional school admission interviews, appearance is very important. You want to look and act like a professional. Listen carefully to the questions that you're asked and avoid gum chewing and smoking. Make good eye contact (but don't stare!). Sit in a relaxed but alert position. These points may seem obvious or trivial, but too often failing to pay attention to them means losing a job.

You might be interested in the results of a recent survey of the most common reasons for turning someone down for a job; these are shown in the next box.

Common Reasons People Are Turned Down for a Job

- **Inability to express him/herself clearly**

- **No clear purpose**

- **Poor appearance**

- **Lack of interest in the company**

- **Unwilling to start at the bottom**

- **Too interested in making money**

- **Limp handshake, poor eye contact**

- **Lack of courtesy, maturity, or tact**

Keep these reasons in mind as you prepare for your own interviews.

Now Just Where Are All These Jobs?

If you've stayed with us up to this point, you know about all of the important steps in job hunting but one—locating the jobs themselves. In this section we'll discuss a number of approaches for you to consider.

Campus Placement Office

Most college campuses have a **placement office**, often a part of the career center, where notices of job openings are posted. A wide range of employers know that college campuses are a good source of new employees, so the placement office can be an important resource for you.

On-Campus Recruiting

Employers that traditionally hire large numbers of new college graduates sometimes send recruiters directly to campuses to interview candidates in person. The placement office will be able to give you the schedule of recruiters on your campus, as well as helpful information about the process as a whole. If your interests and background match one or more firms that are recruiting on campus, the results can be excellent — they have jobs and are actively recruiting you! Be sure to check the schedule *early* in your senior year because there may be a small number of interview slots for each position.

Personal Referrals

Friends, family, neighbors, and professors often know about jobs and can tell you about them. Be sure to let people know you are in the job market and what kind of job you are interested in. This method can be very effective.

Classified Ads

Although only a small percentage of job vacancies is advertised in this way, it is worthwhile to keep an eye out for particularly interesting jobs. Remember, though, that a classified ad can receive hundreds of responses so don't be disappointed if the results from this approach are not spectacular. Just be sure to put most of your efforts into the other methods.

Mail Campaign

It can sometimes be helpful to send a cover letter and résumé to companies you might be interested in even if you don't have a personal referral or know of a particular job opening. Personal contacts are the best way to go about this, but it is not always possible, particularly when you are interested in firms that are some distance away.

Government Jobs

Federal, state, city, and county jobs offer a wide range of opportunities. Most require some sort of exam that is offered only at certain times, e.g., the Civil Service exam. The career advising office on your campus can give you information about exam dates. Once you have your test scores, you must then contact relevant agencies directly for jobs. The whole process can be very time consuming so it is important for you to allow yourself time (no less than three to six months in general) and to be patient.

Professional Journals

Journals and newsletters can often help you identify jobs in particular fields; many such publications have a classified job openings section. These can be good leads in some areas, especially highly technical fields.

Employment Agency

We leave the job-hunting method most people tend to think of first — the employment agency — for last in our discussion. Employment agencies are clearinghouses for jobs and perform their service for a fee, obtained either from you or a potential employer. If you use the services of an employment agency, be sure you understand who has to pay the fee before you accept any referrals from them. In general, if you follow through with the other methods we've listed above, you shouldn't need to use an agency at all.

In summary, remember that job seeking requires time and energy, and really good jobs are rarely found overnight. You can help yourself along by being organized in your search and by presenting yourself in the best possible light in your résumé, letters, and interview. Few people get job offers by sitting passively near their telephone or mailbox — an active, informed approach is what's needed.

Suggested Readings

Bolles, R. N. *What Color is Your Parachute?* Berkeley, CA: Ten Speed Press, 1981.

Koberg, D., and Bagnall, J. *The Revised All New Universal Traveler—A soft-systems guide to: creativity, problem-solving, and the process of reaching goals.* Los Altos, CA: William Kaufmann, Inc., 1981.

Manpower Research Associates. *Arco Handbook of Job and Career Opportunities.* New York: Arco Publishing, Inc., 1978.

Yeomans, W. N. *Jobs '80 '81: Where they are and how to get them.* New York: Perigee Books, 1979.

14.

Some Final Words

What we've tried to do in this book is to tell you some of the things we've learned about how to get the most out of college—knowledge we've acquired from psychology, from our own experiences, and from our students.

What we'd also like to do, of course, is grab you by the shoulder, look you straight in the eye, and say, "*Try* some of the things we suggest, they work!" Unfortunately, we can't follow you around encouraging you to take our advice. Besides, it would be against our main message: "*You* take charge of your life."

If there is one thing we want you to take away from this book it's the idea that you can do a lot to determine what's going to happen to you. We want you to believe that if things are not going the way you want, you can almost always do something to change them.

This is especially hard to remember when you find yourself in a complicated situation like college, and everything is coming at you at once. But even if you are at the point where you're overwhelmed, it's almost always possible to dig in your heels, pause and say "wait a minute," and then take a look around. Usually, when you do you will find changes you can make.

Once you pinpoint the problem, the change is often simple. For example, you may need to study in the library during hours when it's noisy at home. Sometimes the change can mean a lot of work for you such as making a better social life for yourself or learning new study skills. Sometimes, when you see things have gotten way beyond you, the best thing you can do is yell "Help!" and grab a lifeline from the counseling service.

While doing these things may be hard, letting events push you around rarely gets you where you want to be. You may not get everything you want out of college, but a lot of what you do get is, or can be, under your control.

Our book is a good place to start practicing this way of doing things. Not all of our advice is good for everyone: not everyone has the same problems or can use the same solutions. You have to do the picking and choosing, deciding which of the problems we talk about are yours and which of our solutions, if any, are worth trying. After you've given it some thought, you may decide to just live with some problems—that the effort you would need to solve them wouldn't be worth the payoff. What we do hope, of course, is that before you leave a problem unsolved (and this is sometimes the better choice), you face the problem, take it apart, and think through the steps you *could* take to solve it.

"You take charge of your life" is an important message, even if things are going *well* for you. Don't forget, good can always get better, and probably easier.

If you have any ideas we haven't included or problems and solutions we haven't thought of, or if you think some of our advice is awful (or even if you like the book as it is), we'd like to hear from you.

Meanwhile, good luck, good choices, and good future.

Appendix

Kinds of Colleges

Specific facts about particular colleges are easy to find — college catalogs and guidebooks are full of them. What is more difficult to find, though, is some overview of what different types of colleges are like. In this Appendix we will tell you something about various kinds of colleges and how their differences might affect you.

If you are going to college for the first time and are trying to choose among several or if you are thinking of transferring, the information below may help you decide. Keep it in mind when you visit campuses (always a good idea if possible) or are reading the material sent to you. Even if you are happily in your third year somewhere, thinking about these features can help you place your school in some overall scheme and call your attention to things you may not be taking advantage of.

Institutions of higher education can differ in many ways.

Four-Year vs. Two-Year

In 1980, approximately two-thirds of all undergraduates in the United States were enrolled in four-year colleges. Four-year colleges award the B.A. (Bachelor of Arts) and B.S. (Bachelor of Science) degrees. Two-year colleges (sometimes called junior or community colleges) award the A.A. (Associate of Arts) or A.S. (Associate of Science) degrees. Currently, it looks as if a larger and larger percentage of college students will attend two-year schools. All the information in this chapter is relevant to four-year colleges and much applies to two-year institutions as well. (The special opportunities and problems of two-year colleges are covered in Chapter 10.)

Universities vs. Colleges

A university is generally a large institution that offers both undergraduate and graduate degrees (see Chapter 13). In contrast, a college is usually a smaller school specializing in undergraduate education. This difference, though, does not apply in all cases: St. Lawrence University, for example, has undergraduate programs only, while Boston College gives graduate degrees. The terms are not always used consistently!

To confuse matters even further, a university is sometimes made up of a collection of schools or colleges. For example, the College of Arts and Sciences, the College or School of Engineering, the Law School, and the Medical School on a particular campus might be part of a single university, but each might have a separate admissions policy. In this case, "college" does not mean undergraduates only. In this book, we use the words college and university interchangeably.

Public vs. Private

This distinction refers to where the college's money comes from. Public colleges are supported by state or local tax money as well as, in many cases, by students' tuition. Since tuition in public colleges is generally quite low, however, public colleges must rely heavily on tax dollars for their existence. Their operation depends on the public's continued belief that more good than harm is done to society and to students by going to college. The amount of money available to the school depends on how much money the state legislature has available and how willing it is to spend some of it on higher education. Faculty and administrators at state colleges and universities spend a lot of time worrying each year about what the legislature will do to their budget.

Private colleges depend on students' tuition and on private money (donations) rather than public money (taxes). Even though tuition at a private college may be several thousand dollars a year, it usually pays less than half the cost of a student's college education. The rest comes from large and small gifts from **alumni** (former students), wealthy individuals, corporations, and foundations. Some gifts are used directly to pay part of the costs of running the college, and some are included in the college's **endowment,** money or property that is invested or rented for the income it produces. Obviously, the college wants to spend only the income produced and to avoid spending the endowment itself, or there will be no money left to earn money. Public colleges are happy to receive donations as well, but gifts usually play a smaller role in paying bills. Faculty members and administrators at private colleges spend many hours worrying about the rate of return the endowment is earning and whether alumni support is shrinking.

Rich vs. Poor

As implied in the last section, both public and private colleges can be relatively well off, or on the brink of financial disaster. This affects you in many ways. The quality of the faculty can depend on how high the salaries are, and faculty morale is affected by what the professors think about the school's future. Money also determines, to some extent, such things as the size of the library, how up to date the computer facilities are, how often the dorms are cleaned, and the amount of financial aid available.

Open Admissions vs. Highly Selective

An institution that has truly "open admissions" would admit anybody who wanted to learn. Most open admissions schools require at least a high school diploma. The idea behind open admissions is that everyone should have a chance (no matter what their past record) to show that they are able to do college-level work. Most two-year colleges and some four-year colleges have open admissions.

Highly selective institutions base their admissions on past performance such as high school grades and SAT scores. For example, if a student has done better than 95% of the other students in high school and on national exams designed to measure basic verbal and mathematical ability (e.g., SATs), then it is a good bet that they already have much of the information, many of the skills, and the level of interest in learning that is needed for success in college.

Highly selective colleges also differ somewhat in what they consider important information about you, besides your academic record. For example, some more selective schools will count it in your favor if you are the son or daughter of an alumnus, are from a state or ethnic group they feel is underrepresented on their campus, have shown some unusual talents, or have experience gained through jobs or volunteer service.

Most four-year colleges fall somewhere in between having open admissions and being highly selective.

Traditional vs. Experimental

Colleges also differ in the way they approach education in general. In most college courses taught in the United States, students and professors meet together in the classroom for several hours a week. The professor lectures; there is some discussion; and the student reads, writes a paper perhaps, and takes exams. Each term, the student takes several courses like this, with the courses running pretty much independently of each other.

Experiments in education have produced many other possibilities. For example, at some colleges the student concentrates on a single issue taught from several points of view (e.g., scientific, historical, philosophical) rather than taking several separate courses per term. The student may write many more papers and take fewer exams than in the traditional college. Students may meet individually with faculty members in **tutorials** to discuss readings and the papers they have written instead of going to formal classes. Finally, written evaluations rather than letter grades are used at some experimental schools.

Urban Location vs. Rural or Small-Town Location

Some colleges are in the center of huge cities, some in the suburbs, and some are surrounded by fields and woods. Where your college is located will be important to your extracurricular life.

The advantage of an urban college is that there are many exciting things to do off campus. Compared to a rural campus there are more movies, plays, churches, restaurants, discos, museums, music—more of everything including other campuses. Extracurricular cultural events are likely to be at a more sophisticated level than you would find in a small town. There is probably good public transportation; you are nearer airports, trains, and several highways, making weekend or vacation trips to other places much easier. All of this means that off-campus excitement is easy to reach and does not require a lot of planning. This can be an important part of a college education and of your growth, but this easily available entertainment can also tempt you away from your books.

The disadvantages of an urban college can be expense, crime, and a lack of peace and quiet. Off-campus living in a city is almost always more expensive than in a small town. Even if you live at school you will still eat and shop off campus often—probably more than you would at a rural campus. Many of those wonderful cultural events cost money (of course, some are free) and are hard to pass up. If you are moving to the city from the country, be prepared for unexpected expenses.

An advantage of a rural college is the relaxed and often beautiful setting. Rural colleges may have a much more peaceful (and cleaner!) air, and campus activities will probably be more important in your extracurricular life than they would be at a city college. This doesn't mean that nothing happens off campus in small towns. Things do, but they are likely to be connected with schools and churches and to be family-oriented. Rural colleges are often near good spots for outdoor activities — mountains, lakes, and beaches. If you have any interest in outdoor activities this is a good place to learn more.

The disadvantages of the rural college can be isolation, boredom, and the difficulty of adjusting to a more relaxed life if you come from a big city. Life at a small rural college can become very ingrown.

Religious vs. Secular

Many colleges were originally founded and funded by religious groups. In some cases the relationship to the religious groups has continued at a high level, in some it has disappeared, and in some it is maintained in only a few ways with little direct effect on the students (for example, there may be a ruling that the majority of the trustees be from the founding religious denomination). Secular schools, on the other hand, may never have had a religious connection and were started by state governments or by individuals.

Schools with a strong connection to a certain religion are likely to demonstrate this by having an additional set of rules. These requirements will differ from school to school, depending on what people of that religion believe. Some colleges forbid drinking, smoking, dancing, or card playing; others require daily or weekly attendance at chapel. At some colleges, stimulants, such as coffee, tea, or cola drinks, may not be sold. At others, only kosher food may be available. There may be dorm curfews, dress codes, or required religion classes. Saturday classes may be forbidden. All of these rules are less likely at a secular college. If you are attending a college that has religious connections (check the catalog), it is a good idea to find out in advance what the rules will be.

If you are going to a college connected with your religion, this can be a help to you in following your faith, especially if the requirements of your religion are unusual in the rest of the country. This is not just a matter of resisting temptation, but also of how much time and effort you have to spend; if you go to a secular school and have to search all over town for a kosher meal or the right kind of chapel, this will take time from your studies. You would also have to make up classes your religious holidays require you to cut. If you don't dance or drink it may be easier to find comfortable social events at a college with your own beliefs. It is also easier to feel comfortable with people who think and act like yourself (not that all people of one religion are alike, but they at least agree on certain beliefs and behaviors).

On the other hand, college is supposed to expand your horizons. Most secular colleges are pluralistic, meaning they have many kinds of people from many different religions. It often helps to understand your own faith when you compare it with others. You may never think seriously about why your religion requires or forbids certain foods or activities or clothes until you are able to see that there are other ways of doing things. As we note in Chapter 8, college is a time when many people find, strengthen, or lose their religious faith. A secular college can be a challenging experience.

Small vs. Large

People usually think about the size of a school in terms of how many students are registered in any given year, rather than how many faculty or buildings or acres it has. As a rule of thumb, a "small" college has under 5000 students, and a "large" college has over 20,000. Because the number of faculty hired does not go up at the same rate as the number of students admitted, when there are more students there are larger classes, at least during the freshman and sophomore years. Smaller classes do not necessarily have better lectures, but you will probably be able to get more individual attention from faculty if you have special problems. You may be more likely to write papers, have class discussions, or have essay exams (all of which are very important in building your communication skills). At a small school, you may not get to know more people, but those you do know will be a higher percentage of the total. Thus, at a small school you may feel more like everyone belongs to the same community.

On the other hand, large colleges tend to have a wider range of courses, activities (bands, theater groups, visiting celebrities), and facilities. Also, a large school is more likely to have major competitive sports programs that can help create community spirit. The pressure to conform to any particular social or political viewpoint is probably less. There are more potential friends to choose from, and being anonymous gives a special kind of freedom that may be attractive to you. The sheer size and number of activities going on around you can also be exciting.

With and Without Graduate Programs

Almost all four-year colleges award bachelor's degrees, but some also have graduate programs. Generally, you must have an undergraduate degree before you can work toward an advanced degree. Master's (M.A. and M.S.) and doctoral (Ph.D.) degrees are those most frequently offered; medical (M.D.) and law (LL.D. and J.D.) degrees are others. Why do we bother to mention graduate degrees when this book is supposed to be about you, the undergraduate? It turns out that the presence of graduate programs has consequences for your undergraduate education that may not be obvious at first.

When a college has graduate programs, the undergraduate must share the spotlight with the advanced students. Graduate education usually has two closely related parts—classwork and involvement in creative scholarship or research. Since these activities require a lot of a faculty member's time, professors will generally teach fewer undergraduate courses and perhaps have somewhat less time for the undergrads. As a result, undergraduate classes may be larger, and students may have fewer opportunities for personal contact with faculty.

There are some things that make up for these disadvantages. Professors who teach graduate courses are usually deeply involved in research themselves, and this can be good for undergraduate education. Research, by the way, means much more than white lab coats and test tubes. A sociologist may do research with questionnaires, a historian may try to understand a past event by reading old documents, and a literature professor's research may be an analysis of a particular author's work. A music professor may compose, and a poetry professor may write—but all of this is scholarly work or research.

In any case, people who are active in research of their own may bring their enthusiasm for their work with them to the undergraduate classroom. Textbooks that give nothing but one set of facts after another can cause students to wonder why any reasonable person would spend his or her life studying a particular topic. But learning from someone who can show you firsthand the excitement of discovery or creativity in a field can bring a subject to life.

A second advantage of learning from faculty who are doing research is the opportunity to become a part of that research. Many faculty members welcome advanced undergraduate students in their research programs. This kind of experience can be the high point of your undergraduate years and can help you make career choices.

If you are a student at an institution with graduate programs you will probably soon meet "T.A.'s." The initials stand for **teaching assistant**, a graduate student who either helps a faculty member in a course or teaches an entire course him/herself. (Sometimes these people are not called T.A.'s but section leaders or graduate assistants.) Working as a T.A. gives graduate students an opportunity to earn some money, as well as gain experience doing what many of them hope to do as a career—teach. Surprisingly, very few graduate programs that prepare people to be college teachers actually give courses in how to teach; these skills are usually learned by doing.

Most teaching assistants are eager to do a good job. While they don't have as much experience as the average faculty member, they often more than make up for this with hard work and enthusiasm. Also, not long ago they too were undergraduates. This may make them more understanding. On the other hand, they may remember their own tendencies to goof off and may demand even more from you. It is hard to generalize!

A Word About Prestige

Almost everyone is at least vaguely aware that academic institutions differ in prestige. Prestige cuts across all of the things we've talked about before. What is the basis for differences in reputation? You might think prestige depends on how selective a college is in its admissions procedure. If a college receives many more applicants than it can accept, it can afford to be highly selective in its admissions requirements. This can't be the whole answer, though, because there are several highly respected state universities that are required by law to accept any high school graduate in the state who wants to attend. Also, this answer may be a little like putting the cart before the horse—*why* do some colleges get more applications than others? One reason, of course, is their prestige, but we have now come full circle in our reasoning.

Basically, a college's reputation depends on how well-known its faculty members are and/or what people think about its educational programs. At smaller colleges emphasizing undergraduate education, the reputation of individual faculty as scholars may not be as important as the type and quality of the programs students can take. At research-oriented colleges and universities, the research accomplishments of faculty members are more important in determining prestige. Most colleges are not good at everything. A college might have an excellent program in French and a weak program in physics, or vice versa. Usually, the more good departments a college has, the higher its prestige.

Index

About the Authors

Marcia K. Johnson, a professor in the Department of Psychology at the State University of New York at Stony Brook, received her undergraduate degree, as well as her Ph.D. in experimental psychology, from the University of California at Berkeley. She has eleven years of teaching experience at SUNY Stony Brook and was director of its undergraduate program in psychology. A member of the Committee on Scientific Awards for the American Psychological Association, she has done extensive research in the area of comprehension, learning, and memory.

Sally P. Springer, an associate professor in the Department of Psychology and assistant provost at SUNY Stony Brook, received her B.S. from Brooklyn College and her Ph.D. in experimental psychology at Stanford University. She has nine years of university teaching experience and has acted as director of the Psychology Department's Honors Program at Stony Brook. The American Psychological Foundation awarded her a Distinguished Contributor Award for her book (coauthored with Georg Deutsch, 1981) *Left Brain, Right Brain.*

Sarah Hall Sternglanz is an adjunct assistant professor in the Psychology Department and a lecturer in women's studies at the State University of New York at Stony Brook. She received her undergraduate degree from Radcliffe College and her Ph.D. in developmental psychology from Stanford University. She has headed the undergraduate psychology program at Stony Brook and has been involved in other student advising activity. Her research has centered on women's problems related to traditional sex roles in the academic and business worlds.

About the Illustrator

Steve Bjorkman is an artist and illustrator from Irvine, California. His college-oriented drawings originated while he attended Trinity College in Deerfield, Illinois, and produced a cartoon strip for the campus newspaper. Currently working with his brother at the Bjorkman Bros. Card Co., he also exhibits his drawings and watercolors at various galleries and art festivals.